From Rhetoric to Reform?

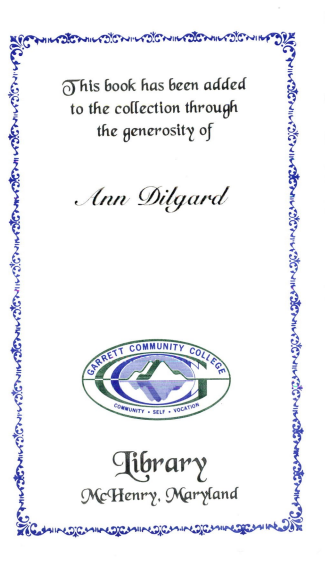

Dilemmas in American Politics

Series Editor   **L. Sandy Maisel,** *Colby College*

Dilemmas in American Politics offers teachers and students a series of quality books on timely topics and key institutions in American government. Each text will examine a "real world" dilemma and will be structured to cover the historical, theoretical, policy relevant, and future dimensions of its subject.

BOOKS IN THIS SERIES

From Rhetoric to Reform?
Welfare Policy in American Politics,
Anne Marie Cammisa

The New Citizenship: Unconventional Politics, Activism, and Service
Craig A. Rimmerman

The Angry American: How Voter Rage Is Changing the Nation
Susan J. Tolchin

No Neutral Ground? Abortion Politics
in an Age of Absolutes, Karen O'Connor

Onward Christian Soldiers? The Religious Right
in American Politics, Clyde Wilcox

Payment Due: A Nation in Debt, A Generation in Trouble,
Timothy J. Penny and Steven E. Schier

Bucking the Deficit: Economic Policymaking in the United States,
G. Calvin Mackenzie and Saranna Thornton

"Can We All Get Along?" Racial and Ethnic Minorities in
American Politics, Paula D. McClain and Joseph Stewart Jr.

Remote and Controlled: Media Politics in a Cynical Age,
Matthew Robert Kerbel

FORTHCOMING TITLES

Making Americans, Remaking America:
Immigration and Immigrant Policy,
Louis DeSipio and Rodolfo O. de la Garza

Two Parties—Or More? The American Party System,
John F. Bibby and L. Sandy Maisel

The Dilemma of Congressional Reform,
David T. Canon and Kenneth R. Mayer

From Rhetoric to Reform?

Welfare Policy in American Politics

Anne Marie Cammisa
Suffolk University

Westview Press
A Member of the Perseus Books Group

Dilemmas in American Politics

Copyright © 1998 by Westview Press, A Member of the Perseus Books Group

Published in 1998 in the United States of America by Westview Press, 5500 Central Avenue, Boul-der, Colorado 80301-2877, and in the United Kingdom by Westview Press, 12 Hid's Copse Road, Cumnor Hill, Oxford OX2 9JJ

A CIP catalog record for this book is available from the Library of Congress.
ISBN 0-8133-2995-7 (hc) — ISBN 0-8133-2996-5 (pbk)

The paper used in this publication meets the requirements of the American National Standard for Permanence of Paper for Printed Library Materials Z39.48-1984.

10   9   8   7   6   5   4   3

To my grandparents:
Massimo Vincenzo and Rosina (Cichetti) Cammisa
and John Joseph and Annie (Clancy) Hitchman

Contents

1 Introduction: Why Is Welfare a Dilemma for American Politics?

• •

2 A Brief History of Welfare in the United States

• •

3 Welfare Reform in the Policymaking Process

• •

4 Welfare Policy in American Politics: From Rhetoric to Reform   95

5 Implementation and Beyond: The Present and Future of Welfare Reform   123

Illustrations

Tables

Figures

Acronyms

ADC	Aid to Dependent Children
AFDC	Aid to Families with Dependent Children
BBA	Balanced Budget Act
CETA	Comprehensive Employment and Training Act
EITC	Earned Income Tax Credit
EOA	Economic Opportunity Act
FAP	Family Assistance Plan
FSA	Family Support Act
GA	General Assistance
HHS	Department of Health and Human Services
NGA	National Governors' Association
PRWORA	Personal Responsibility and Work Opportunity Reconciliation Act
SSA	Social Security Act
SSI	Supplemental Security Income
TANF	Temporary Assistance for Needy Families
WIN	Work Incentive Program
WRA	Work and Responsibility Act

Preface

On July 26, 1996, I went to the Capitol Building to watch the Senate vote on the Personal Responsibility and Work Opportunity Reconciliation Act (PRWORA), the welfare reform bill that had already been approved by the House. The vote was a foregone conclusion. In fact, two very similar bills had already passed the House and Senate but had been vetoed by President Clinton. Since he was sending signals that he might sign the bill, Republicans and Democrats alike wanted to jump on the welfare bandwagon, especially in an election year when it could become a hot-button campaign issue. As I walked to the Senate gallery to watch the historic vote, I happened upon a forlorn Senator Daniel Patrick Moynihan (D-NY). Senator Moynihan is considered an expert on welfare and was instrumental in writing and passing the last version of welfare reform. He is also a difficult person to classify, having been a New Deal Democrat early in his career, later becoming a "neoconservative" who worked on Nixon's welfare reform bill, and now being called one of the last liberals on welfare reform. As I passed him, I said good afternoon, and like the good politician that he is, he stopped and shook my hand. When I thanked him for his efforts on the welfare bill, he looked at me and put his hands in the air. His face betrayed emotion, and he was silent for a moment until he finally mouthed the words "We lost." A moment later, I was in the visitors' gallery of the Senate, sitting next to a couple of tourists who clapped and cheered quietly (the Senate has rules of decorum that apply even to visitors) every time a senator's remarks mentioned cracking down on welfare cheats. They high-fived when the bill passed.

The conflicting emotions betrayed by the senator and the tourists illustrate the dilemma of welfare reform. Senator Moynihan has gone on record numerous times lamenting the end of the guarantee of government assistance to poor families, a guarantee that has existed since the New Deal and that was eliminated when the PRWORA was passed. The senator believes that the government has a responsibility to care for its poorest citizens and that the PRWORA abdicates that responsibility. But the tourists sitting next to me in the gallery were convinced that welfare is a bad program, prone to cheating and abuse. They had no doubt heard from politicians—liberals and conservatives alike—that welfare causes dependency, that welfare recipients find it easier to accept government money than work, and that the system itself has done nothing to eradicate poverty and may in fact exacerbate it. They were ecstatic when the Senate voted to end the entitlement status of welfare; they believe such a move will end the dependence of poor people on government programs.

Who is right? Should low-income families be guaranteed assistance from the government? Or does such a guarantee create an underclass of people who become too dependent on government programs? For sixty years the dominant ideology has been to use welfare to fight poverty. Now the dominant ideology is to end welfare to fight dependency. Although many policymakers are truly interested in creating a welfare system that works, for too long welfare has been used as a political tool. In their competition for middle-class voters, Democrats and Republicans have blamed welfare for everything from illiteracy to the national debt.

I would like to believe that the Republican bill will not only end welfare as we know it but will also alleviate poverty as we know it. However, I am skeptical that this will happen. The first goal is certainly much easier to achieve than the second. Whether ending welfare will have positive effects on those in poverty is yet to be seen. Having worked on evaluations of welfare over the past several years, I know that for welfare reform to work, money needs to be spent—on child care and health insurance for welfare families and on job search activities for welfare parents. I also know that the vast majority of people in this country hate welfare. Working people, particularly low-income workers, resent the system, which seems to "reward" people for not working. Even welfare recipients themselves hate welfare because it is demeaning and saps them of their self-esteem.

The dilemma explored in this book is whether welfare policy can assist the poor without creating dependency. For some reformers, dependency is the problem; for others, poverty is the problem. In my classroom experience, I have found that most of my students view welfare from the perspective of dependency: The students believe that government social programs have created a class of citizens who do not work because it is too easy to receive government assistance. The attitude of my students (which I think is a fair reflection of many, if not most, college students today) is problematic for people who have studied the issues of welfare and poverty. Many poverty scholars find "dependency" to be a loaded term. In this book, I intend to explain why some people believe that welfare causes dependency, while others believe that focusing on dependency moves us away from the real problem of welfare reform: ameliorating poverty. Although I do not believe that eliminating the federal guarantee of assistance is the best way to reform welfare, I do understand the concerns that many Americans have about the existing welfare system. What is needed now is a dispassionate discussion of why poverty exists, what role the government should play in eliminating it, and how best to encourage individual responsibility.

This book is a first step. I have endeavored to give a fair presentation of the various perspectives on welfare reform (although like any other author, my biases come through from time to time). My hope is that both those who agree with Senator Moynihan and those who are champions of the Personal Responsibility and Work Opportunity Reconciliation Act can find some food for thought.

I would like to thank the many people who made this book possible. First, my colleague Dr. John Berg deserves credit for suggesting to series editor Sandy Maisel and to me that I write this book. Sandy Maisel, Jennifer Knerr (the former Westview editor), and editor Leo Wiegman were enthusiastic supporters of the project. I would especially like to thank the anonymous reviewers who provided insightful comments and valuable recommendations for revision. I also had excellent research assistance from three graduate students at Suffolk University in Boston: Michele O'Connor and Jennifer LaPierre, who diligently searched for, photocopied, and summarized articles on welfare reform, and Heather Rowe, who cheerfully dug up statistics and stories about people on welfare. My students at Suffolk also deserve credit for helping me think out loud about welfare in class and for listening patiently while I explained (again) why the difference between a block grant and an entitlement program is so important. A visiting scholarship at the Murray Research Center at Radcliffe College opened up the vast resources of the Harvard University library system to me. I would also like to thank Senator Herb Kohl, for whom I worked during my APSA congressional fellowship year in Congress. Although he and I disagreed about the appropriateness of the block grant approach to welfare, I enjoyed our lively discussions about the issue.

Thanks also go to my friends and former colleagues at the Urban Institute, with whom and from whom I learned about welfare policy: Demetra Nightingale, Pamela Holcomb, Carolyn O'Brien, Barbara Cohen, Sue Poppinle, Regina Yudd, Kristin Seefeldt, Mildred Woodhouse, Sanya Drumgoole, and especially the late Lee Bawden, whose kind and gentle manner is greatly missed.

Finally, my family, as usual, have been ardent champions of my work. My uncle, John Cammisa, has been telling his friends in Waterbury, Connecticut, about the book his niece is working on. My parents, Guido and Mary Ida Cammisa; my aunt, Katharine Thomas; my brothers, James and Michael Cammisa; my cousin, Laurie Cammisa; and my husband's parents, Joaquim and Barbara

Manuel, have provided support, encouragement, and patience as I worked on this project. My husband also provided all of these—and he read the manuscript, offering helpful suggestions. Thanks to Dr. Paul Christopher Manuel, whose love and devotion made this book possible.

Anne Marie Cammisa
Boston, Massachusetts

1

....

Introduction:
Why Is Welfare a Dilemma
for American Politics?

We all know that the typical family on welfare today is
very different from the one that welfare was designed
to deal with 60 years ago. We all know that there are a
lot of good people on welfare who just get off it in the
ordinary course of business, but that a significant
number of people are trapped on welfare for a very
long time, exiling them from the entire community of
work that gives structure to our lives.

President Clinton, August 22, 1996

W hy is welfare a dilemma in American politics? How can something intended to help be viewed as a problem? Let's start from the beginning. What is welfare? The dictionary gives two definitions. The first says that welfare is "the state of doing well, especially in respect to good fortune, happiness, well-being, or prosperity." If that's what welfare is, then why does everyone complain about it so much? The second definition gives a clue: "of, or relating to, or concerned with welfare and especially improvement of disadvantaged social groups." Even though this definition is closer to what comes to mind when we hear the word "welfare," it's still not quite what politicians and citizens mean when they use the word. In fact, looking at the first definition, it's clear that "welfare" has positive connotations—"well-being" and "happiness"—but when we hear the word on the nightly news or use it in discussions with friends or colleagues, welfare has an obvious negative connotation. What's wrong? Why are there two polar opposite ways to use the same word?

The problem is that a government program that was intended to do good, to provide for the well-being of citizens, doesn't seem to have done what it set out to do. And so when people use the term welfare in political discussions, they are describing a social policy that nobody seems to like. Welfare no longer means well-being; it means government social programs to help the poor. And those programs are widely viewed to be a failure. Some people believe that social programs not only haven't helped the poor, but that they have actually hurt them by encouraging behavior that keeps people from taking responsibility for themselves. So welfare no longer conjures up images of prosperity and well-being, but of government spending on poverty programs that don't help the poor.

> In two generations the meaning of welfare has reversed itself. What once meant well-being now means ill-being. What once meant prosperity, good health, and good spirits now implies poverty, bad health, and fatalism. . . . Today, "welfare" means grudging aid to the poor, when it once referred to a vision of the good life.[1]

There is another piece missing from the puzzle. We can assume that policymakers would not set out to create a hugely unpopular program. No politician wants to tell taxpayers that he or she is wasting their money on policies that can't or won't work. So the question is how did welfare become a bad word—how is it that policies intended to do good have instead engendered controversy and derision? Were the original policymakers hopelessly idealistic? Did they engage in an elaborate attempt at social engineering doomed to failure from the start? Or has welfare become a scapegoat for all of society's ills? Are politicians waging "class warfare" by attacking programs designed to help the disadvantaged?

There is some truth to all of these theories. Today's welfare programs were designed in the 1930s during the **New Deal** and expanded in the 1960s during the **Great Society**. Although they attempted to solve societal problems of the time, current social conditions have changed drastically, making many welfare law provisions obsolete or counterproductive. Aid for Dependent Children (ADC), the New Deal welfare program created in 1935, was originally intended for widows with children, creating the requirement that welfare go only to families in which one parent was absent, a requirement that seems today to discourage family values. On the other hand, as detailed in Chapter 2, American society has always had an interest in helping its least well-off citizens. In addition, the poverty rate today is much lower than it was in the 1930s, when welfare was originally introduced, or in the 1960s, when welfare was significantly expanded. Some contend that this is evidence that the New Deal and Great Society programs have accomplished their goals; others, that the low poverty rate is only the result of an underclass dependent on government spending to stay out of poverty.

Definition of Terms

This book will employ the word "welfare" in its common usage: to describe the federal-state poverty program formerly known as **Aid to Families with Dependent Children (AFDC)** and first introduced as Aid to Dependent Children. President Clinton signed the **Personal Responsibility and Work Opportunity Reconciliation Act (PRWORA)** on August 23, 1996; the legislation ended AFDC, replacing it with a block grant aimed at the same population. The new block grant program is called **Temporary Assistance for Needy Families** (TANF). Most families that qualified for AFDC also qualified for food stamps (vouchers used to make food purchases) and Medicaid (medical care); under TANF, there is overlap between these programs as well. Therefore, these programs are also generally included in a definition of welfare. Not included in definitions of welfare are other programs that, like AFDC and TANF, use governmental spending to provide for the well-being of a specified group of individuals. For example, social security provides for retired individuals who have paid social security taxes. Prior to social security, old age was a primary cause of poverty. Now social security helps out that formerly disadvantaged group. We don't call it welfare; we call it "social insurance," in part because the program is paid for by a payroll tax. The government also provides education assistance in the form of college loans, which again are not called welfare because they go in large part to the middle class, and the usual connotation of the word welfare refers to programs aimed at people in poverty.

Although social security was also intended to eradicate poverty, it is viewed as being vastly different from other poverty programs. Older people are not expected to work, and so most people believe that they deserve some assistance from those of us who can work. Throughout our history, public opinion has made a distinction between the worthy (or deserving) and unworthy (undeserving) poor. **Worthy poor** are defined as the people who are poor through no fault of their own. Generally, those people we consider worthy poor have fallen into poverty because of age, temporary unemployment, or disability. We think of them as being truly needy. The **unworthy poor**, on the other hand, are those whom society sees as responsible for their own poverty, or at least as capable of getting themselves out of poverty. The unworthy poor are the able-bodied poor—young adults who have no obvious disability to keep them from working. Obviously, not everybody agrees that distinctions should be made about the "worthiness" of people in poverty. In addition, even if one wants to make such distinctions, it is often difficult to differentiate between the truly needy and able-bodied poor. Widowed mothers—in particular, white middle-class widowed mothers—were more likely to be considered truly needy in the earlier history of AFDC because they were not a visible part of the workforce. Since mothers at all income levels now work, welfare mothers with no obvious disabilities are now regarded as able-bodied or undeserving poor. But what about the children of those mothers? Although most people agree that these children deserve assistance— they are poor not through their own fault—it is not clear how we can best help them. And most Americans believe that those children should be provided government assistance, even if their parents have been cut from the welfare rolls. (See Table 1.1.) The underlying premise of the new welfare reform law is that encouraging parents to work will help their children in the long run. What will happen to children whose parents are unwilling to work, unable to find full-time jobs, or unable to sustain a job because of the expense of child care is not clear.

The so-called unworthy poor are the poor who society now believes have become *dependent* on welfare. Popular opinion is that the availability of government cash assistance to poor families makes it easier for them to take ad-

TABLE 1.1   Public Opinion and Children on Welfare

Should the government provide separate benefits to children whose parents' benefits have been cut off?

Should	78%
Should not	17%
No opinion	5%

SOURCE: *The Gallup Poll, 1994* (Wilmington, DE: Scholarly Resources, 1995).

vantage of welfare than to take responsibility for their own lives. The program doesn't seem to provide enough incentives for individuals to work. The word "dependent" is a controversial term with respect to welfare. Nobody says that social security recipients are dependent on their checks, despite the fact that many would be in poverty without them. To use "dependent" to describe poor people is, in the eyes of critics, a way of objectifying them. And not everybody agrees that welfare causes dependence. Welfare is a response to poverty, and poverty may be caused by a variety of factors. From the 1930s until very recently, poverty was viewed as a *structural* problem. According to this theory, the structure of our economic system leaves some people behind. To call them dependent on welfare is to blame them for something over which they have no control. Structural definitions of poverty are not currently popular. Today, the welfare debate centers on individual failings as the cause of poverty. This view of poverty as an *individual* problem harkens back to earlier times in our country's history, from the colonial period to the early twentieth century.

The structural definition of poverty gave us the concept of a **safety net**. Picture an acrobat walking a tightrope. She has confidence that she will not fall, but just in case, there is a net underneath, to catch her in the event of an accident, perhaps saving her life. In welfare policy, working Americans are the acrobats, confident that they can make it on their own. The safety net consists of government programs to catch them if they fall, programs such as AFDC (now TANF), unemployment insurance, and social security. Almost everyone agrees that there should be a safety net in the United States. But whether current programs act as a safety net or discourage people from trying to make it on their own is a point of contention. One person's safety net is another person's dependency trap. By the 1990s, AFDC had become the target of attacks from both sides.

> Today, a consensus that the AFDC program does not really help poor children spans the political spectrum. Conservatives believe that AFDC destroys initiative and creates perverse incentives that discourage work and marriage. Liberals contend that it offers inadequate benefits while robbing individuals of their dignity and self-esteem.[2]

There is an old saying about welfare, first popularized in describing work relief programs during the Great Depression, that it should be a "hand, not a handout." In other words, welfare should offer assistance to help people make it on their own, rather than providing an easy excuse for not working. The use of this phrase has been extended to apply to today's welfare mothers—who in 1935 were not expected to work, but who today are required to do so. Was the old AFDC a handout rather than a hand? Will changing the law actually help single mothers to find a job and make it on their own? No one knows for certain.

Myths About Welfare

The word "welfare" is a powerful symbol. It evokes images of people taking from the government without contributing to society. It conjures up feelings of resentment among working poor struggling to make ends meet without taking welfare and among middle-class Americans who feel that they bear the tax burden for those receiving benefits. It comes with a *stigma* attached: that people who accept government poverty assistance are at best, misguided and at worst, lazy, conniving, and cheating. This stigma is real and intentional. In our society, which is based on a capitalistic system, we want to encourage values of hard work and individualism. Nonetheless, welfare has been unfairly maligned ever since its inception. The resentment among the general public is real, but some of the perceptions about welfare are not. This section addresses seven myths about welfare, myths that have some basis in reality but that also contribute to the acrimony surrounding the debate about welfare. Most of the myths arose because of problems in the AFDC program. This section will examine those myths in the context of AFDC; later chapters examine in depth how TANF changes the AFDC program.

Myth 1: Welfare Causes Poverty

The AFDC program has been attacked as the cause of poverty in the United States. This claim in and of itself is unjustified. Poverty existed long before AFDC and will continue to exist long after AFDC has been eliminated. Figure 1.1 shows the poverty rate for selected years from 1896 to 1992. (The poverty rate is the percentage of people whose incomes fall below a defined minimum level of subsistence.) AFDC, like other welfare programs, was specifically designed to alleviate poverty. The real question is not whether welfare causes poverty, but whether or not it actually helps those in poverty. There is considerable debate about this question. Many people believe that welfare programs, whatever their intentions, created negative incentives for people in poverty, making their situations worse rather than better. The argument goes something like this: Because AFDC historically went to single-parent families and because benefit levels increased based on the number of children in a family, it encouraged out-of-wedlock births. Because AFDC required people to have very low income and asset levels, it discouraged work. Moreover, some politicians argue that the very existence of poverty programs discourages individual responsibility. It is unfair to help people who are not working, while the working poor are trying to make it on their own.

In Figure 1.1, governmental assistance was included in determining income. Therefore, some people believe that the calculated poverty rates are too low, since some families' incomes rose above the poverty level only because they had received government money. The controversy centers around the question of dependency. Can we say that poverty programs are successful when they provide families with enough income to take them out of poverty? Or are they only successful when the families can make enough money on their own to bring their incomes above the poverty level? In previous decades, when the structural definition of poverty was popular, the fact that government assistance added enough money to family incomes to bring them above the poverty level was a sufficient measure of success. Now, when we focus on individualism, such assistance is said to cause dependency.

Although not everyone agrees that welfare causes dependency, even among those that subscribe to this view, there is no agreement as to how to foster independence while still helping the poor. The only sure way to eliminate dependence on government programs would be to eliminate those programs entirely, and most politicians do not want to do that. Despite our concerns about personal responsibility, most Americans believe that the government should play at least some role in aiding the poor. As shown in Table 1.2, although a significant number of Americans believe that welfare spending should be reduced, only about 10 percent believe that it should be ended entirely. And although most Americans don't like welfare, they still believe the government should help the poor. In a 1994 poll, 62 percent of the public favored decreasing spending on welfare, while 59 percent favored increasing spending on helping the poor. Thus, while Americans hate the welfare system, they are not opposed to its underlying premise of assistance.[3] At previous times in our history, we have concentrated on using welfare to provide long-term assistance. The current political environment stresses providing incentives for individuals to use government assistance only as a short-term, last resort.

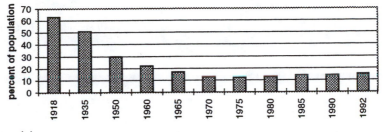

Figure 1.1
Poverty rate, selected years, 1918–1992
SOURCES: For years 1896–1965, James T. Patterson, *America's Struggle Against Poverty,*
1900–1980 (Cambridge: Harvard University Press, 1981), p. 79; for years 1960–1992,
U.S. Congress, House Committee on Ways and Means, *Overview of Entitlement Pro-*
grams: 1994 Greenbook, Appendix H, Table H-4.

TABLE 1.2   Public Opinion on Welfare Spending

	April 1994	*December 1994*
Percent who believe that		
1. Welfare spending should be		
increased	10%	14%
kept at current levels	32	34
reduced	44	36
ended altogether	10	10
No opinion	4	6
2. The entire welfare system should be		
replaced	36%	45%
fixed (but not replaced completely)	63	52
No opinion or mixed response	1	3

SOURCE: *The Gallup Poll, 1994* and *The Gallup Poll, 1995* (Wilmington, DE: Scholarly Resources, 1995, 1996).

Myth 2: Once a Family Went on AFDC, They Usually Stayed on It for Many Years

If families become dependent on welfare, then it stands to reason that they continue to receive welfare benefits over the long run, for many years, or even a lifetime. In fact, a substantial proportion of families continued to receive AFDC for
spells of longer than five years. In one sense, this myth is not a myth at all. If one
looks at the number of people on AFDC at any one moment in time, one finds
that 65 percent of them have been on welfare for eight years or longer. This
clearly shows a trend of long-term welfare receipt, if not dependency on welfare.
However, this statistic can be misleading. If one looks at families that go on and

TABLE 1.3   Duration of AFDC Spells (in percentages)

	Persons Beginning First "Spell" on AFDC	All Persons on AFDC at a Given Point in Time (snapshot picture)
Expected duration of AFDC spell		
1–2 years	30	7
3–4 years	20	11
5–7 years	19	17
8 or more years	30	65

SOURCE: U.S. Congress, House Committee on Ways and Means, *Overview of Entitlement Programs: 1994 Greenbook.*

off of welfare over a longer period of time—say ten or more years—one finds that a large number of families have been on welfare for shorter "spells" of four years or less. "Although most 'spells' of AFDC are relatively short, most persons enrolled in the program at any point in time are in the midst of spells that last at least eight years."[4] Many families actually receive benefits for a couple of years, become self-supporting for a couple of years, and then return to welfare for various reasons (loss of a job, the breakup of a marriage). Are these people dependent on the system? They seem to use it frequently. On the other hand, maybe they are using welfare as a "safety net," that is, they try to make it on their own, but when they cannot, they rely on welfare for short periods of time. Perhaps these families are "deserving poor" who need welfare to assist them occasionally.

Table 1.3 illustrates the difference between a snapshot picture of duration of welfare spells and a longer-term analysis, by predicting the expected length of time on welfare for those beginning a spell on AFDC and for all those currently receiving benefits. Sixty-five percent of those receiving benefits at any one time would end up as long-term recipients (eight years or more), but 50 percent of those just starting on AFDC would have been off in less than five years. Box 1.1 explains this seeming contradiction.

The welfare reform mandates that families cannot stay on welfare over the long run, by limiting the amount of time any one family can be on welfare to a lifetime total of five years. In addition, within two years of receiving benefits, the head of any welfare household (with some exceptions) must enter into employment. Republicans and Democrats alike hope that this will reduce dependence on welfare. No one is sure what the cost of that reduced dependence will be. Advocates for the poor argue that reducing dependence comes at the cost of eliminating large numbers of families with children from the welfare rolls, families that may become homeless and may not have enough money to provide the most basic necessities for their children.

BOX 1.1   HOSPITAL BED ANALOGY

The House Ways and Means Committee uses the following analogy to explain the difference in the expected length of time on AFDC for persons just beginning their first spell and for those already on AFDC.

> An example of spells of hospitalization will help to establish this point. Consider a 13-bed hospital in which 12 beds are occupied for an entire year by 12 chronically ill patients, while the other bed is used by 52 patients, each of whom stays exactly 1 week. On any given day, a hospital census would find that about 85 percent of patients (12/13) were in the midst of long spells of hospitalization. Nevertheless, viewed over the course of a year, short-term use clearly dominates: out of the 64 patients using hospital services, about 80 percent (52/64) spent only 1 week in the hospital. Exactly the same dynamic accounts for the results with regard to welfare experience. One of the most important lessons from the longitudinal evidence is that while the welfare population at any point in time is composed predominantly of long-term users, the typical recipient is a short-term user.

SOURCE: U.S. Congress, House Committee on Ways and Means, *Overview of Entitlement Programs: 1994 Greenbook.*

Myth 3: Welfare Is the Cause of the Federal Deficit

The federal deficit exists because the government spends more money than it receives in revenues. If AFDC, food stamps, and Medicaid were eliminated entirely from the 1996 federal budget, the federal deficit would still exist, as shown in Table 1.4. There is, of course, room for debate about whether welfare funding is well-spent money. But to blame the federal deficit entirely on welfare is simply wrong. The government spends money on a variety of services, including, among other things, farm subsidies, student loans, defense, and education. The deficit is a result of the combination of all government spending. All budgeting involves prioritizing. Do we want to spend less or take in more? If the government would like to reduce the deficit, it must either raise taxes or cut government spending. Such decisions require difficult choices among competing programs. The president and Congress will reduce spending on welfare with the PRWORA, cutting the welfare budget by about $55 billion over five years. Yearly savings amount to more than $10 billion per year, which still doesn't reduce the federal deficit significantly. Eliminating the deficit will require cuts in more than just welfare spending.

TABLE 1.4   Government Spending on Social Programs, 1992 (in millions of dollars)

Total federal budget	1,128,518
Total deficit	340,490
Total federal spending on AFDC, Medicaid and food stamps combined	179,746
As percent of total federal budget	15%

SOURCES: U.S. Bureau of the Census, *Statistical Abstract of the United States, 1995;* Executive Office of the President, *Budget of the United States Government: Historical Tables, Fiscal Year 1995.*

Myth 4: Most of the Money Spent on Welfare Is for Adults

Whether or not this assertion is true depends upon your definition of welfare. As noted earlier, the common usage of the word "welfare" describes the block grant replacing the Aid to Families with Dependent Children program, which gives assistance to families. In order to qualify, an adult must have a child. Benefits are determined based on the number of individuals in the household. The welfare check goes to the parent to pay for support of his or her family. **Food stamps**, which provide vouchers to purchase food, also go mostly to families. **Medicaid** funds also go to poor families, although the majority of Medicaid expenditures are for long-term care for the elderly poor. Poverty programs that are aimed at adults include **Supplemental Security Income** (SSI), some of which also goes to children, and **General Assistance**, which is paid for by the states.

If, when we say welfare, we mean AFDC or the block grant that replaces it (as we usually do), then it is not true that most beneficiaries are adults. There has been a much larger number of children than adults receiving AFDC because eligibility for the program was based not only on income, but also on the presence of a child or children in a family. Table 1.5 makes clear that more children than adults received AFDC in 1992, with almost 70 percent of the benefits going to children.

Welfare generally refers to AFDC (now TANF) not because the aid goes to children, but because it also goes to the able-bodied adults who are the primary caregivers for those children and who are often considered to be dependent on government aid. In contrast, SSI and old age assistance, which also provide cash assistance to the poor, go to the disabled and the elderly, who are generally believed to be deserving of such aid. Social security, discussed in Chapter 4, is not considered cash assistance, but rather social insurance, and is not called welfare. "Federal assistance to the elderly has been universally accepted. Why? Because the aged are not expected to work. So the trade-off between work and benefits does not arise."[5] General Assistance, which is also directed at able-bodied

TABLE 1.5   Children and Adults in Poverty and Receiving AFDC, 1992 (in millions)

	Number in Poverty	Number Receiving AFDC	Number Receiving AFDC as % of AFDC Population
Under 18	14.6	9.2	67.7
18 and over	22.2	4.4	32.3
Total	36.8	13.6	100

SOURCE: U.S. Congress, House Committee on Ways and Means, *Overview of Entitlement Programs: 1994 Greenbook,* Appendix H, Table H-1.

adults, is not included in discussions of the federal welfare system because it is a state-run program, administered in only 23 states.

We do spend money providing for the welfare of adults, even though we don't call it welfare spending. Table 1.6 shows the amount of federal spending on cash assistance programs for adults and children as well as for social security, which is called a social insurance program since it is funded by payroll taxes paid by its recipients. As Table 1.6 indicates, a large number of adults receive monetary assistance from the government—the largest group of these being social security recipients. If we were to classify all of the programs listed in Table 1.6 as welfare programs, then it would be fair to say that more adults than children receive welfare benefits. However, if by welfare we mean AFDC, then the opposite is true. And, as Table 1.6 makes clear, there were more than three and a half times as many adults receiving social security (about 35.6 million) as children receiving AFDC (about 9.6 million) in 1993.

Myth 5: Most Welfare Families Are Black

In fact, most families receiving welfare benefits are *not* black (African American). In 1992, about 37 percent of the families receiving AFDC were headed by a parent who was African American, which means that about 63 percent of welfare families were headed by parents who were not black (see Table 1.7). There are more white families on welfare than black families: In 1992, nearly 40 percent of all welfare recipients were non-Hispanic white. About 18 percent of welfare families were Hispanic, so it would be true to say that more minority families (55 percent) receive welfare than non-Hispanic white families. In addition, as a proportion of their total population, more blacks are on welfare than whites. As of 1994, approximately 14 percent of all the children in the United States were on AFDC. However, about 40 percent of all black children were on AFDC, compared to 30 percent of Hispanic children and only 7 percent of white children.[6]

TABLE 1.6   Adult and Child Recipients of Federal Cash Assistance, 1993 (in thousands)

Cash Assistance Programs Aimed Primarily at Adults	
SSI (includes some children)	5,984
Old Age Assistance	16
Aid to the Permanently and Totally Disabled	28
Total	6,028
Aid to Families with Dependent Children	
Adults	4,659
Children	9,598
Total	14,257
Social Insurance for Adults	
Social Security	35,585

SOURCE: U.S. Bureau of the Census, *Statistical Abstract of the United States, 1995.*

TABLE 1.7   Race of Parents in AFDC Families, 1992 (in percentages)

White	38.9
Black	37.2
Hispanic	17.8
Native American	1.4
Asian	2.8
Other and unknown	2.0

SOURCE: U.S. Congress, House Committee on Ways and Means, *Overview of Entitlement Programs: 1994 Greenbook.*

Race is a thorny issue in American politics, an issue that impacts welfare policymaking. In the welfare debate, liberals have often accused conservatives of racism, saying that attacks against welfare are designed to bring out negative feelings about blacks among working-class whites. Some people believe that using the word "welfare" itself is a powerful racist symbol and that attempts to cut back the welfare state are poorly disguised attacks on the black "underclass." For their part, conservatives accuse liberals of race baiting, saying that any attempt by conservatives to discuss valid issues such as the rise in out-of-wedlock births or family breakdown is instantly labeled racism. It is no surprise that intelligent discussions about welfare are often left by the wayside over the issue of race. "The long-term legacy of coupling social policy to racial issues has diminished America's ability to stem the decline of the inner cities and to protect the family."[7]

Myth 6: Prior to the New Deal, the Government Did Not Spend Money on Welfare, Leaving It to Private Charities

From the beginning of our country's history, the government has spent public money on the provision of welfare. Public agencies dealing with poverty have existed since colonial times, often acting hand in hand with local governments.[8] However, governmental spending occurred at the local and state levels, rather than at the national level. At the time of the New Deal, state, local, and charitable spending was insufficient to care for the large number of people in poverty, and the federal government stepped in. It is true that governmental spending has increased greatly over the course of our country's history, as is evident in Figure 1.2. But welfare has long been viewed as a governmental function. As demonstrated in Chapter 2, welfare in the United States can trace its roots to Elizabethan England, and the government has made provision for welfare since colonial times. As historian Michael Katz notes, "American public welfare has a very old history. Public funds have always relieved more people than private ones. Voluntarism never was and never will be an adequate answer to the problem of dependence."[9]

Complaints about spending on welfare are usually aimed at federal spending. The system of federalism, one of the innovative features of American government, has sparked debates about the proper level of government to implement a variety of social programs, not the least of which is welfare. In the 1930s, the federal government took on more authority over welfare, and in the 1990s, the federal government is ceding its authority—at least partially—to

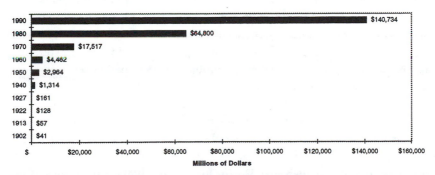

Figure 1.2
Total Government Spending on Public Welfare: 1902–1990
SOURCE: George Thomas Kurian, *Datapedia of the United States, 1790–2000: America Year by Year* (Lanham, MD: Bernan Press), 1994.

the states. The question is whether the federal government is equipped to solve problems that may (or may not) be handled better by the state governments.

Myth 7: Most Welfare Families Have Lots of Children

In fact, as Table 1.8 shows, the average welfare family consists of three people. In other words, the average welfare mother has two children. This has been true since the late 1970s. The reason for the misperception is unclear, but it probably has to do with the fact that welfare benefits increased with the number of children in a family. A family that had more children received a higher AFDC benefit. Some people believe that this fact influenced a woman's decision to have more children while on welfare. Others contend that the amount of money paid for each additional child was so low that it would hardly be worthwhile to have another child—whose additional expenses would more than outweigh the additional benefits received from AFDC. The average amount that a family received in additional benefits for having three children rather than two was $72 per month in 1994.[10]

One other issue with respect to childbearing is the number of children born out of wedlock. The illegitimacy rate for welfare families is much higher than the national average because eligibility for AFDC historically was tied to single parenthood. (Until 1961, in order to receive benefits, an AFDC family had to be either headed by a single parent or include a parent who was unable to work due to incapacitation. In 1961, AFDC eligibility was extended to families in which one parent was unemployed.) In 1939, 50 percent of the families on AFDC were headed by widows or included two parents.[11] In 1975, about 56 percent of AFDC families were headed by divorced or separated parents, and about 33 percent were headed by never-married mothers. By 1994, almost 66 percent of all AFDC families were headed by never-married mothers, 30 percent by divorced or separated parents, and 2 percent by widows.[12] In contrast, approximately 13 percent of all single mothers in 1976 had never been married; this proportion increased to about 36 percent in 1992.[13] Despite the fact that AFDC had a larger proportion of never-married mothers than the rest of the population, the proportion of never-married mothers has been growing at a faster rate in the population as a whole (at all income and age levels). The percentage of never-married mothers on AFDC doubled from 1975 to 1994 (from 33 percent to 66 percent). During approximately the same time period, the percentage of all mothers who have never been married nearly tripled (from about 12 percent to about 36 percent).

TABLE 1.8   Average Family Size, Selected Years, 1969–1986

Year	*Average Number of Persons in AFDC Household (includes parent(s) as well as children)*
1969	4.0
1973	3.6
1975	3.2
1979	3.0
1983	3.0
1986	3.0
1988	3.0
1990	2.9
1992	2.9

SOURCE: U.S. Congress, House Committee on Ways and Means, *Overview of Entitlement Programs: 1994 Greenbook.*

Problems with Welfare

There are two competing philosophies that underpin American ideas about social welfare policy: individualism and community. The first focuses on the ability of an individual to succeed in a free market economy. In a capitalistic society, individualism and free choice are valued, and the government is expected to intervene as little as possible in the economic decisions of individuals. Too much government interference stifles creativity and innovation and encourages laziness. The value of individualism is apparent in many of the beliefs and myths we have about American society. To take just one example, the Horatio Alger stories each featured a young boy in poverty who, through hard work and perseverance, rose above his situation and became a success. The second philosophy, community, posits that individuals must take responsibility for one another. The idea of community is based on the Judeo-Christian tradition that runs through much of American social thought. Those who are well-off have a responsibility to take care of those who are less fortunate. As a community, if one of our number is in difficulty, we are under an obligation to help him or her. Community begets charity. We see evidence of this tradition when Americans across the country respond to a crisis such as an earthquake in California or the Oklahoma City bombing. Television news stories often show people traveling from faraway points to help out those who have experienced tragedy, and the president usually sends federal assistance in the form of money or services to alleviate the situation.

In some instances, it is easy to see where individualism ends and community begins. When independent, hard-working individuals fall upon hard times, as did many Americans during the Great Depression, most people would agree that the community should help them, that they are deserving of assistance. When an individual who has worked a lifetime and raised a family finds money short at retirement age, most of us believe that society has some sort of obligation to help him or her. On the other hand, if a person isn't elderly, has no physical problems, and yet doesn't work and has no money, many of us believe that he or she should learn to take care of himself or herself, that society doesn't have an obligation when individuals refuse to help themselves. But what if that person has children? Should the value of individualism include them, or should they be taken care of under the value of community? Or what if there are some extenuating circumstances that make it difficult for the individual to hold down a job? Under what circumstances should the community feel an obligation to help? These are some of the difficult questions that welfare reform must answer.

Reducing dependency encourages the American value of individualism. Everyone should be able to get ahead, and government should not get in the way of individual achievement, either by placing too many barriers in front of a person or by coddling them. Helping the poor focuses on the American value of community, which has not been as strong as individualism. Helping the poor might also mean that there is a structural problem with the economic system that requires government intervention; this is incompatible with the value Americans place on capitalism. We can agree in a time of crisis (the depression, for example) that the government has an obligation to help the poor because it is easy to see the crisis as the cause of poverty. Large-scale government programs are less popular when the public doesn't perceive a crisis; thus the War on Poverty of the 1960s never achieved the popularity of the New Deal, in part because poverty was not as visible in the 1960s as it had been during the early 1930s. In fact, the relief programs created during the depression were acceptable *because* they were temporary (the very word relief implies short-term action). The New Deal relief programs became work programs later in the 1930s and were eventually abandoned when employment increased during World War II.

Because of our emphasis on individualism, it is hard for Americans to believe that able-bodied people who have been in poverty for long periods are poor through no fault of their own. Taken from an idealistic point of view, this disbelief reflects the American can-do spirit, the idea that anybody can get ahead through hard work and spunk. Taken from a cynical point of view, this disbelief belies the American sense of community and betrays an underlying tendency to blame the poor for their own poverty. The cynical point of view also posits that this disbelief is perpetuated by those who hold money and power, since it discourages any attempts at redistribution of wealth in society and maintains a compliant working class. "To buttress weak market controls and ensure the availability of marginal labor, an outcast class—the dependent poor—is created by the relief system. This class, whose members are of no productive use, is not treated with indifference but with contempt."[14]

An additional problem complicating welfare policy is the sense that somehow the budget could be balanced if only we could figure out the best way to take care of the poor. And those who argue for reducing dependency often are also the ones arguing strongly for cutting the costs of welfare. However, reducing dependency is expensive because it necessitates changing the behavior of the poor. The cheapest, simplest way to relieve poverty is to provide assistance: Give cash to the poor to level out their incomes, without requiring extensive eligibility investigations (which increase bureaucratic expenses) or asking recipients do something in return, such as engaging in work or training. (There are administrative costs associated with ensuring they actually do the work or training and with actually providing the service.) But helping the poor by providing cash assistance does not reduce their dependency on government programs (defining dependency as the necessity to receive government help in order to stay out of poverty). And therein lies the dilemma. If we help the poor, we run the risk of creating dependency on government programs; if we don't help them, we can't be sure that they will take themselves out of poverty. Perhaps both sides are right. Government programs cause dependency and the structural problems in the economy make such programs necessary.

The Dilemma:
Can We Help Those in Poverty Without Causing Dependence on Government Programs?

Does society have an obligation to help its least well-off citizens? From colonial times to the present, Americans have believed that it does and that the government should have some hand in providing poverty assistance. The question throughout our history has been who deserves this assistance, and making that determination has been the sticking point in welfare policy. Poverty can be viewed as a structural problem (caused by forces beyond individual control) or as a cultural problem (caused by a lack of personal responsibility on the part of the poor person). In our society, which reveres rugged individualism, self-help, and the value of hard work, it is difficult to justify providing welfare to people who could be taking care of themselves. Thus, the distinction between the worthy and unworthy poor serves a useful purpose: We should provide government assistance to the worthy but make such assistance undesirable for the unworthy poor. The central dilemma in American welfare policy has always been how to help the truly needy while discouraging the able-bodied poor from relying on governmental assistance. In the current political environment, the dilemma is phrased in terms of dependency. The able-bodied poor are viewed as dependent on governmental programs. We would like to create a system that somehow teaches these people to be independent, to rely on themselves rather than on the government. Thus the dilemma is how to help the poor to achieve self-reliance without causing dependence on government programs.

The dilemma is further complicated by the fact that it is difficult to determine how much of poverty is caused by individual failings and how much is caused by structural factors. Is it reasonable to believe that all able-bodied citizens have the capacity to keep themselves out of poverty? Or should we simply accept that a certain number of people will fall through the cracks in a capitalistic economy and provide cash assistance to them? If the old welfare system created incentives to engage in "undesirable" behavior (accepting assistance rather than working, having children without a father present), can we be certain that we are capable of creating a system with incentives to do the opposite? Is government the appropriate vehicle for changing social behaviors?

These are questions which get at the heart of the welfare dilemma: What can we expect of government assistance to the poor? Is simply eliminating poverty through cash assistance enough? Or must we ensure that the poor are capable of rising out of poverty—and eliminating "undesirable" behaviors—on their own? And how much should the government involve itself in the personal lives of those who accept government assistance? By framing the dilemma in terms of helping the poor or reducing dependency, this book will examine the question of what government assistance can (and should) do. There are many who believe that the real problem is not dependency, but poverty and that the PRWORA ignores the fact that there are structural, economic, and social problems that create and maintain poverty. Instead of focusing on the factors that lead to dependency, they believe the government should focus on the factors that lead to poverty. Blaming the poor for their "dependence" on government assistance, they say, only worsens their plight. And the poor, as the least likely group of the population to vote, are an easy target. Politicians can manipulate the middle class, already burdened by taxes, to blame the poor for all of society's problems. As one welfare mother put it:

> We already have very little self-esteem, so the last thing we need is to have the country turn around and point the finger at us and say we're the problem, but suddenly we're responsible for everything from the schools to the deficit. It's like ethnic cleansing. That's what it feels like.[15]

Those who believe that poverty is a structural problem and that government should concentrate on helping the poor rather than reducing dependency are in a minority. The tide of opinion about welfare has shifted to the right, at least among policymakers in Congress and the executive branch. It is no longer acceptable, as it has been at other times in our history, to blame the economic structure for the problem of poverty. The current view is that individual failings have been exacerbated by government programs that make it too easy for people to accept assistance. So the question has become how to re-create those government programs to encourage individual responsibility and independence. Proponents of the welfare reform act would argue that reducing dependence on government programs is the same thing as helping the poor. They believe that limiting the ability of individuals to obtain and stay on government assistance will encourage them to find work and take responsibility for themselves and their families.

Can the government help the poor by reducing their dependence on the very programs it provides for their assistance? This is the goal of our latest attempt to reform welfare. If previous history serves as a guide, we will always have difficulty using government programs to change the behavior of individuals.

The remainder of this book places the welfare dilemma in its historical and political context. Chapter 2 provides a history of welfare reform, tracing its roots to Elizabethan England, and demonstrates the difficulty we have always had in defining who should get government assistance and what the proper role of that assistance should be. Chapter 2 also examines the New Deal and the War on Poverty, government programs that were initially intended to relieve and eradicate poverty, respectively, and that have become the objects of recent attacks on the welfare system. The chapter thus explains how the political and economic environments influence our response to the problem of poverty. Chapter 3 examines how welfare fits into the policymaking process. In this chapter, I describe the political environment that led to passage of the PRWORA, trace the bill's somewhat precarious route through Congress, and demonstrate how election year pressures led to a sweeping reform of the welfare system. Chapters 4 and 5 look at the present and future of the welfare system in American politics. Chapter 4 first provides an overview of AFDC, the welfare program in the United States for the last sixty-one years, and then explains how the PRWORA, which went into effect in October 1996, changes welfare policy. Chapter 4 asks the question, how did the debate about welfare reform move to the right? Chapter 5 features an in-depth analysis of the PRWORA and a discussion of its major provisions, as well as an examination of the initial implementation of the act. Chapter 5 then looks at the future of the welfare dilemma, examining how incrementalism and change go hand in hand.

2

A Brief History of Welfare in the United States

W hen we think of the history of welfare in the United States, we usually start with the time period following the Great Depression. Certainly, President Franklin Delano Roosevelt's New Deal created what we currently refer to as welfare: federal assistance to poor families and their children.[1] The New Deal also created **social insurance** programs such as **unemployment compensation** and social security—programs which have had much more political popularity than public assistance to poor families. But the roots of welfare go back much further in our history than the New Deal. Indeed, the colonists brought the very idea of public assistance with them. One could say that the welfare program in the United States dates all the way back to Elizabethan England, when the idea of a public obligation to assist the poor was codified in the poor law. However, since colonial times, the perception of what is the best method of assisting the poor has undergone many changes.

Vigorous debates over the proper role of government in providing welfare have occurred throughout U.S. history. Throughout these debates, several dilemmas have emerged. First, there has been a constant tension over who is responsible for poverty—the individual or the structure of society. Is poverty an individual problem? In that case, government assistance should be limited in order to encourage individuals to work their way out of hard times. Is poverty a structural problem? In that case, society as a whole (the community) has an obligation to care for those who fall into destitution. Another dilemma in the welfare debate is the question of who deserves to receive aid. Throughout history, society has attempted to divide the poor into two categories: those who are truly needy and those who are capable of taking care of themselves. Making the determination of who fits into which category has created difficulties. Related to both of these dilemmas is the proper role of government in providing welfare: Should welfare benefits be a right that individuals can expect from the government, or should welfare be a method by which the government attempts to change undesirable behavior?

The form that welfare takes depends upon what we expect it to do. There are at least four ways that the government can try to alleviate poverty: through prevention, rehabilitation, assistance, or deterrence.[2] Government programs can be used to try to prevent poverty from occurring in the first place, by targeting groups of people who are likely to fall into poverty. Government programs can be used to rehabilitate the poor, in order to change their behavior. Rehabilitation and prevention are related, but rehabilitation focuses on changing undesirable behavior. The government can alleviate poverty by simply providing assistance: giving money to those who are below a certain income level, without expecting any behavioral change. Finally, government programs can be used to deter people from asking for assistance. The idea is to make welfare itself so undesirable that very few people would want to ask for it in the first place. Each of these ideas (prevention, rehabilitation, assistance, and deterrence) has been tried at one point or another in our history; each has achieved limited success. In some cases, two ideas have been tried at the same time, often at cross-purposes.

Let us now travel through the history of welfare, starting with its roots in the Elizabethan Poor Law.

The Roots of Welfare: From the Elizabethan Poor Law to Colonial America

Elizabethan Poor Law

Public welfare began in England as a response to an economic problem. During the 1500s, the British feudal system was breaking up. Feudalism had given each individual a role to play, based upon economic position. Feudal lords owned the land and parceled out portions of it to peasants (or serfs), who received a place to live and subsistence levels of crops in exchange for farming the land for the feudal lord, who reaped huge profits from the work of the serfs. There was no way for a peasant to get ahead in the system, but the feudal lord provided some protections against old age and poverty. In the 1500s, the feudal system fell apart as England became more and more commercial. The economic system changed, and power went from the feudal lords to the emerging merchant class. Rather than having a land base, the economy became wage-based. The working class was no longer tied to a piece of land, but rather to a job that provided a wage. And such jobs were less stable than land. People moved from job to job and often fell into periods of destitution. Even so, despite huge differences in class and income, there was still some sense of interconnectedness in society, and the upper classes felt the need to provide some security for those in the lower class who were unable to support themselves when they were out of work. Of course, this limited security was not necessarily created out of the goodness of the hearts of the ruling class. Conveniently, public assistance could also be used to control the labor market and fend off unrest.[3]

At about the same time that the economic system was changing, there were changes in the social structure as well. In a dispute with the pope, Henry VIII closed down all of the monasteries in England, which had not only political and religious implications, but social and economic implications as well. For many years, the monasteries had been the primary source of assistance to those in poverty, acting as way stations or halfway houses. In fact, the government collected a tithe from its citizens which was given directly to the monasteries for the purpose of assisting the poor.[4] When the monasteries closed, thousands of poor people streamed out of them and into the cities, where they, like everyone else, had to compete for wage-based jobs in the new economic system.

The poor were very visible in the cities, and the government needed to expand the assistance it already provided for them. The Elizabethan Poor Law of 1601 codified the form that this assistance would take. It required punishment for those who refused to work. It established the rights of the needy to assistance and it required localities to provide for the poor.[5] Later amendments to the poor law also established the principle of "less eligibility": that cash assistance should be less than the prevailing wage, in order to make work more desirable than public assistance.[6] The poor law defined three different types of poor. The first type consisted of children, who were generally given an apprenticeship so that they could be cared for in the short term and learn a craft in order to care for themselves in the long term. The second group of poor were able-bodied adults, who were expected to work and were given jobs in exchange for money to pay for living expenses. The final group consisted of the lame, infirm, old, and blind, who were given food and shelter at public expense.[7] Although the poor law was a watershed event in the history of public assistance, not everyone was in agreement with its principles. Many of the theorists at the time believed that poverty was a "natural state" for members of the working class. They felt that the poor law thus infringed on the rights of the upper classes, who had an unmitigated right to accumulate wealth, even at the expense of the lower classes.[8]

The Elizabethan Poor Law had elements of all of the four goals of welfare mentioned earlier. First, it provided *assistance* to the poor in the form of money. Such assistance went primarily to those who could not take care of themselves, in a form of social insurance. Second, it acted as a *prevention* by giving apprenticeships to children so that they could eventually take care of themselves as adults, preventing them from falling into poverty later. Third, it was a *deterrent,* by requiring able-bodied adults to work for their relief (at less than prevailing wages) and punishing them if they didn't. This deterrent was intended to encourage adults who could find jobs to do so, since receipt of welfare required them to work anyway. In addition, the Elizabethan Poor Law also drew a distinction between the *worthy* and *unworthy* poor. Able-bodied, as *unworthy* poor, were punished if they refused to work in order to receive assistance. This could also be considered a method of *rehabilitation,* changing the behavior of the poor to fit societal expectations.

Colonial Welfare Policy

When the original colonists came to America, they brought with them elements of the Elizabethan Poor Law. Primary among these elements was the idea that the government had an obligation to provide public assistance. This obligation, like most other governmental roles at the time, was viewed as a local responsibility. Local governments were much more important in the early stages of our history (certainly, during the colonial period, the only national government was in England) out of geographic necessity. Travel was difficult and dangerous, and local communities were isolated from one another. The level of government that was most visible and that had the most power was the local government. Thus, the obligation to care for the poor was a community obligation and carried with it responsibilities on the part of the recipient of government assistance. The value of community was evident during the colonial period. Life in the colonies was difficult, and there was a sense of "we're all in this together." Public opinion held that colonists who were destitute were so due to difficult conditions—lack of roads and other amenities, harsh weather, difficulties in tilling the land—not through laziness.

Public assistance programs in the colonies were local programs, paid for by taxes collected for the purpose of providing for the poor. It was common for government funds to be given to families for taking care of the destitute.[9] Geographic isolation in the colonies contributed to the localism inherent in public assistance and also encouraged the ideas of self-sufficiency and rugged individualism.[10] Because conditions in the New World were so difficult, those who were destitute were considered to be truly needy. It is important to note that the concept of *community* extended only to the European immigrants to the New World. The Enlightenment notion of a *contract,* which meant that individuals agreed to give up certain rights to the government in exchange for protection of others, excluded Native Americans and blacks.[11]

Another element of public assistance transplanted from England was the idea that family members should be responsible for each other and that government assistance should be provided only as a last resort. In both Elizabethan England and colonial America, an impoverished person applying for assistance would first be sent to his or her relatives, who were expected to care for their own. Only if there were no relatives available, or if they were also destitute, was the individual eligible for assistance. Private charity was also used frequently in the colonial days. Wealthier citizens were encouraged to open their homes to the poor, often at public expense.[12] The early welfare system was a tightly woven, local-centered one. In fact, residency laws were strictly enforced. Only residents of a town were considered eligible for the local assistance. Community feelings did not extend far beyond the local area.

Since its very beginning, then, the United States has had governmental involvement in providing assistance to those in poverty. This involvement is a direct result of the British system of public assistance. Localities were the focal point of assistance, families and private individuals were expected to contribute to the care of impoverished community members, assistance only went to members of the community, and a distinction was drawn between the truly needy and those capable of working.

From the Poorhouse to Progressivism

Historian Michael Katz (1986) describes the period between colonialism and the New Deal as falling into two distinct eras with respect to welfare. The first, which he calls the era of the poorhouse, was characterized by a reliance on institutions as a means to care for the poor. He refers to the second era as the construction of a "semi-welfare state," in which protections against poverty were at least partially nationalized and extended. This second era is closely linked to progressivism. As we shall see, attitudes toward the poor changed as the country moved from an agrarian to an industrial economy and, as attitudes changed, so too did the perception of the best method of dealing with poverty.

The Era of the Poorhouse

During the colonial period, local communities provided monetary assistance to those in poverty. Most people also assumed that poverty was due to a lack of available jobs or to an inability to work. As the economy grew, this assumption changed. The general public began to view poverty as being caused by an inherent laziness on the part of the poor. By the nineteenth century, the focus was turned on the poor person as an individual with responsibility for his or her own plight. There were two reasons for this new emphasis. The first was a natural extension of the Enlightenment, a period of great intellectual advancement during the eighteenth century. Enlightenment thought, the political theory upon which our government was based, was concerned with rational and scientific reasoning as opposed to religion or tradition. Humanism was a hallmark of the Enlightenment, which focused on the individual as a human being, with equal rights to other humans. At first, this theory encouraged a sense of community with those in poverty: As equal human beings, the impoverished should be treated with compassion. However, Enlightenment thought also encouraged individualism and personal responsibility and eventually contributed to a belief that the poor were responsible for their poverty, since they had equal opportunities to rise above it.[13]

In addition to political thought, religious thought contributed to the emphasis on personal responsibility. Religious movements of the nineteenth century, including Calvinism, revivalism, and the Second Great Awakening, emphasized individualism, discouraged idleness, and elevated the role of work. The Protestant "work ethic" preached the value of work in molding individuals and creating a productive society. The individual was held responsible for overcoming his or her own poverty through work.[14] Indeed, the Protestant work ethic put forth an "ideal type" who, in addition to working hard,

> is not distracted by activities unrelated to his work, defers for the future all possible rewards for prestige and economic success to be achieved in a later time, conserves his assets and belongings for a time of need for himself and his extended family, saves surplus wealth for the purpose of extending economic enterprise, even at the expense of self-denial in the present.[15]

This increased emphasis on personal responsibility led to an increased importance of the goal of *rehabilitation* of the poor. The way to take people out of poverty was not simply to give them monetary assistance, but instead to provide them with the means by which they could take responsibility for their own well-being. During the colonial period, most poor people had been assisted by "**outdoor relief**"—charity given to them in their own homes, outside of an institution. Gradually "**indoor relief**," or institutional assistance, began to play a larger role. At the start of the nineteenth century, society had four general ways of dealing with the poor: They were auctioned off to the highest bidder; they were contracted out to work in order to cover the costs of their assistance; they were given public charity (outdoor relief); or they were sent to institutions, variously known as **poorhouses**, almshouses, or workhouses.[16] By the middle of the century, public officials saw institutionalization as the best of the four methods of dealing with the poor. The first two, auctioning or contracting, were obviously excessively cruel. The third, outdoor relief, did not require enough responsibility on the part of the recipient, who officials thought would be coddled by the excess charity. The fourth option, the poorhouse, provided assistance and much more. It also acted as a deterrent and a force for rehabilitation.

The poorhouse was the means by which poverty would be eliminated or at least greatly reduced. In the mid-nineteenth century, charitable organizations and reformers were concerned with the problem of **pauperism**. Pauperism describes poverty as an inherently immoral condition. Attempts to alleviate poverty were seen as discouraging work and encouraging dependence on public assistance. The word and the concept it describes is somewhat similar to the "underclass" that politicians and the media talk about today, although the term was more explicit in its judgment of the poor as sinful. The way to discourage pauperism was to make relief less desirable. There was a sense that somehow individuals in poverty found it easier not to become self-reliant if charity were readily available. The argument is remarkably similar to today's indictment of the welfare system. Not only did charity encourage dependence, it also cost the government too much money. Reformers today want to reduce dependency and costs by having states enforce work requirements. Nineteenth-century reformers thought the way to reduce dependency and costs was to provide for the poor through a system of poorhouses, which were themselves a sort of work requirement.

The **scientific charity** movement of the 1840s provided the rationale for the rise of the poorhouse. Scientific charity viewed the poor as individuals who could be molded and changed to become productive middle-class citizens. The way to mold citizens was to force them to work, and institutions were the vehicle to do this.[17] Scientific charity viewed outdoor relief negatively: It encouraged laziness and discouraged the work ethic among the poor. If one could receive public funds for not working, why would one be interested in work? The poorhouse created a way out of this problem. An individual who sought assistance went to an institution where he or she was given work. Women as well as men who entered the poorhouses were expected to work, as they had been since colonial times.[18] The poorhouse was a *deterrent* from accepting relief: The conditions were thought to be so bad that any kind of job would be preferable to going to the poorhouse. Yet at the same time that the poorhouse was to deter the poor from asking for assistance, it was also expected to be a force for *rehabilitation*. The poorhouse taught the work ethic and, in theory anyway, created solid, hardworking citizens. The conflicting goals of rehabilitation and deterrence gave the poorhouses an impossible task: "The almshouse was to be at once a refuge for the helpless and a deterrent to the able-bodied; it was supposed to care for the poor humanely and to discourage them from applying for relief."[19] Unfortunately, neither goal was sufficiently met.

> Trapped by their contradictory purposes, undercut by poor management and inadequate funds, poorhouses never could find useful work for their inmates or offer the old, sick, and helpless, not to mention the able-bodied unemployed, much more than a roof and escape from death by starvation. Nor did they reduce pauperism or cut the cost of poor relief. In fact, despite the diffusion of poorhouses, the volume of outdoor relief continued to grow.[20]

The concept of pauperism helped justify the institutionalization of the unworthy poor. For example, Charles Burroughs, a Protestant minister, delivered a sermon in 1834 on the opening of a new almshouse in Portsmouth, New Hampshire. He made the distinction between poverty and pauperism, expanding on the idea of the worthy and the unworthy poor. Those in poverty, according to Burroughs, are those who have experienced misfortune through no fault of their own and are thus worthy of assistance. This group could include not only the elderly and the infirm, but also able-bodied poor who fell into hard times through the loss of a job. Pauperism, on the other hand, is a result of bad moral character. Paupers are unworthy of aid, since they brought on their condition by their own moral weaknesses.[21] This distinction helped in deciding who should go to the poorhouse: "Paupers" went to institutions as punishment for their moral failings, and the worthy received outdoor relief to help them through difficult times.

The era of the poorhouse focused on individualism over community, and rehabilitation and deterrence over assistance. The poorhouse era was similar to the colonial era in that aid was still provided locally, but the emphasis was more on discouraging the unworthy poor than assisting the worthy poor. Poverty was not just a problem due to difficult economic conditions, it was the result of pauperism, the moral failing of the poor. The community's interest in poverty assistance went beyond outdoor relief. The community required that the poor adhere to certain standards as a condition of assistance. Poorhouses were run by local governments; it wasn't until the late 1800s that state governments attempted to standardize them.[22]

The Problem of the Immigrant Population

Just as changing economic conditions created the need for the Elizabethan Poor Law, economic conditions of the late 1800s also created the need for new responses to poverty. The end of the Civil War brought a large number of unskilled freedmen (former slaves) to northern cities, just as those cities were industrializing. More people poured into the cities in the form of immigrants, mostly from western and southern European countries. Working conditions were bad, jobs were not always available, and large cities had increasing pockets of poverty. White Protestant city dwellers had a difficult time absorbing the black and immigrant populations into their midst. At their worst, social reformers of the period viewed the new population as subhuman and incapable of being reformed. Even at their best, social reformers often had paternalistic attitudes toward both blacks and immigrants, wanting to rehabilitate them by inculcating middle-class Protestant values to which the poor did not necessarily aspire.

The scientific charity movement, which continued into the late 1800s, included some of the best and worst elements of reformers. By the late 1800s, the movement was producing charity organization societies (such as the Association for Improving the Condition of the Poor, or AICP), which worked with the immigrant poor in the cities. In an idealistic way, the charity organization societies wanted to mold productive, happy citizens from the immigrant population of the cities. Charity workers called themselves "friends" and went into impoverished neighborhoods to investigate conditions and provide helpful suggestions. The movement had noble aspirations: to help the poor overcome their own poverty by teaching them the value of hard work and clean living. Simply giving the poor monetary assistance was not enough. They needed to be educated to conform to societal values. According to Josephine Shaw Lowell, founder of the scientific charity movement,

> the best help of all is to help people to help themselves. That is, that instead of receiving the means of living, men should receive from the benevolent the means of earning a living—that the poor man or woman should have the road cleared so that they may themselves march on to success—that their brains should be released from ignorance, their hands freed from the shackles of incompetence, their bodies saved from the pains of sickness, and their souls delivered from the bonds of sin.[23]

Although the goals of the movement were noble, the "friends" from the charity organizations did not always understand or appreciate the culture of the individuals whom they were supposedly helping, and many of the immigrants resented the intrusion of middle-class reformers. And class and cultural differences led to inevitable clashes between those providing charity and those on the receiving end: "The A.I.C.P. probably loved the poor less than they feared or perhaps even hated them. Their object was not so much to help the poor as to remold them into good middle-class citizens, to make them respectable."[24]

Many of the reformers had evangelism—religious conversion—as their stated goal. Between 1800 and 1860, six million people immigrated to the

United States, most of them German and Irish Catholic poor. American re-formers found the new Catholic immigrants to be lazy, indolent, prone to drink, and far too ready to accept public relief. It was quite easy to classify this group as undeserving of public assistance.[25] Poverty among the new immi-grant class was seen as a moral problem, and reformers attempted to regulate their behavior through religion.[26] As the reformers tried conversion, the Catholic immigrants resented their intrusion, and the Catholic Church even-tually set up its own system of charity, including poorhouses, hospitals, and schools.[27] Many of the Catholic hospitals and parochial schools existing today were created in this time period.

Even with its faults, the scientific charity movement was much more open-minded than **social Darwinism**, which followed it. Attempting to apply Dar-win's theory of evolution to human behavior, social Darwinists reasoned that a process of natural selection would eventually weed out the worst of the poor population. Thus, the best poverty policy was to let the poor fend for them-selves, allowing the best to rise to the top and the worst to eventually eliminate themselves from the population. In effect, the unworthy poor would die off.

Dealings with the new immigrants caused a reexamination of the ideas of community and individualism. In the colonial period, the poor were consid-ered part of the community and indeed were not inherently different from the rest of the community. In the mid- to late-eighteenth century, the poor were separate from the community, differentiated by language, cultural, and racial divides. Social Darwinism brought individualism to its worst possible conclu-sion: Let individuals fend for themselves, and eliminate the undesirables in the process. Scientific charity tried to create a sense of community in the new so-cial order, but its participants were limited in their understanding of cultural and religious differences. Scientific charity attempted to create a community by rehabilitation—forcing foreign-born poor to accept and adhere to societal expectations. What they tried to do was not so much wrong as it was incom-plete. Rather than accounting for cultural and religious differences, they tried to create middle-class Protestants out of poor Catholic immigrants, many of whom resented their efforts. Try as they might to be helpful to the urban poor, the charity organizations couldn't help but appear self-righteous and paternal-istic to the new city population.

Progressivism—The Beginning of the "Semi-Welfare State"

The Progressive Era followed on the heels of the poorhouse movement and embodied a strong reaction against institutionalization of the poor. During this time in the United States, prevention was emphasized, but the focus remained on the work ethic and the distinction between the worthy and unworthy poor. According to James T. Patterson, "They still tried to change the needy—to take the poverty out of people as well as to take the people out of poverty."[28] Progressives focused on problems related to industrialization: child labor, the condition of immigrants, the minimum wage, unemployment insurance, racial justice, and the role of women in the workforce.[29]

Settlement houses were one manifestation of progressivism. Jane Addams started the settlement house movement in the United States with the creation of Hull House in Chicago. Middle-class reformers (mostly recent college graduates) "settled" in poor urban neighborhoods and opened their houses to the local population. Like the charity organization societies, they sought to assist the poor by teaching them practical skills related to housekeeping and child rearing. Settlement house workers also wanted to make the poor into mainstream American citizens and "assimilate" them into the dominant Anglo-Saxon culture.[30] They did this by teaching immigrant mothers to raise their children properly, both in terms of general health and well-being and as good citizens. Their goals were both the prevention of poverty and the rehabilitation of the poor. But class differences between the settlement house workers and the poor women they were trying to help were difficult to overcome, and the workers themselves concentrated on societal and personal goals—sometimes at the expense of the needs of the poor. The middle-class reformers used charity as a form of social control, ensuring that the immigrants would learn the "American" ways of family rearing. The reformers, who were mostly women, also used the settlement houses as a means of personal legitimation and validation.[31] The settlement house women created careers out of promoting motherhood, as did women in other careers such as nursing and teaching.

The settlement house workers, although progressive in their view that the immigrants could and should be brought into the mainstream of American society, were not particularly accepting of what we now call cultural diversity. They insisted on conformity to their ideal of motherhood, even if that ideal conflicted with the expectations the immigrants had for themselves.[32] Community was an underpinning of the settlement house movement; however, the movement, like charity organizations, was a bit too idealistic and tended to romanticize the poor.

> It underestimated the desire of working-class people to get out of rundown neighborhoods and buy homes in the suburbs. It did not consider comprehensive programs of social welfare. In its most conservative guises, it was frankly nostalgic . . . in seeking to implant the countryside in the slum. The goal of community nonetheless

persisted for decades—in groups promoting community organization in the 1920s and again in community action agencies in the 1960s. It remained one of the most durable goals of antipoverty warriors in twentieth-century America.[33]

Settlement houses died out by the 1920s: They did not have enough re-sources to reach many of the poor, and the intended population—immi-grants—was suspicious of their "do-gooderism." Gradually, settlement houses gave way to the new profession of "social work." The social workers (many of whom had been settlement house volunteers) were trained in the many new scientific and professional schools of social work that had sprung up in the early part of the century.[34] Now women making a career out of promoting family and motherhood had a new professional identity.

Although the settlement house volunteers were a bit too idealistic and had romanticized notions of the poor, they did create a new understanding of poverty as a *societal* (or structural) problem rather than an individual prob-lem, an understanding that served as the underpinning of poverty policy from the 1920s until very recently. Their focus on prevention and rehabilitation over deterrence led to the demise of the poorhouse system and helped encourage stable family life among the poor. One of the most negative aspects of the poorhouse era had been its breakup of families in poverty. Parents might be sent to the poorhouse, while their children went to orphanages or, in some cases, were sent to live and work with other families in rural farming commu-nities.[35] Conditions in the poorhouses and orphanages were so bad as to be viewed with terror by many of the immigrants they were supposed to be help-ing. The settlement house movement was at least kinder in that it assisted poor families in their own homes and neighborhoods. The movement also led to in-creased state regulation of local institutions such as poorhouses, orphanages, and hospitals. This regulation moved the primary responsibility for welfare from localities to states,[36] the first step on the road to national involvement in welfare.

While idealistic college graduates were attempting to alleviate the plight of the poor by living among them, the progressive movement was also working through the political system to encourage government action. Progressives wanted to curb the excesses of industrialism by creating laws limiting child labor, providing government subsidies to those who lost their jobs (unemploy-ment compensation), establishing a minimum wage, and instituting old-age pensions for retirement.[37] The Progressive Era upheld the notion of commu-nity and saw poverty as a structural problem. Progressive labor laws gave the government responsibility for problems created by the economic structure.

One of the most important innovations of the progressive movement was the state "mothers' pension," the forerunner of the AFDC program. **Mothers' pensions,** instituted in most states, provided a cash grant for single mothers to help them care for their children. This aid generally had a condition attached to it: The mother must be "morally fit" (usually this meant that she was a widow rather than a "deserted" wife—one whose husband had left her[38]—or never-married mother). Mothers' pension programs rejected the institutions of the poorhouse era, operating on the belief that it was better to provide aid to mothers to enable them to care for their children at home than to place those children in orphanages.[39]

Proponents of mothers' pensions portrayed the single mothers as worthy poor, who needed support to engage in the noble occupation of raising children. Women were viewed as dependent: If the husband and father in a family died, the mother had no means to care for herself and her children. Although many working-class single and married mothers worked, the mothers' pension programs expected the rearing of children to be a full-time job. Aid went to mothers who stayed home and cared for their children, not for day care or job training to help women to work. Like the settlement houses and the scientific charity movement, mothers' pensions were designed as a way to mold the poor into proper middle-class citizens. "In settlement houses, women's organizations, and social agencies, maternalist reformers defined the family as the crucible of Americanism and emphasized the special responsibilities of motherhood to democracy."[40]

Mothers' pensions also set the stage for a conflict that did not fully materialize until almost three-quarters of a century later. By directing assistance to families without fathers, the mothers' pensions specifically left out intact families. Families with fathers present had a built-in wage earner and so were not eligible for assistance. Because they linked aid to the dependency of women, mothers' pensions did not provide assistance for women to become independent. They did not help women to find or maintain jobs; a mother's primary job was to stay at home with the children. They also did not provide aid for families who were still poor despite the presence of a breadwinning father. Mothers' pensions later became the basis for Aid to Families with Dependent Children, which eventually went not only to "worthy" widowed mothers, but to divorced and never-married mothers as well. And, as more and more mothers at all income levels joined the workforce, resentment against the recipients of AFDC built up. Once society had accepted the concept of working mothers, the idea of providing assistance for mothers to stay at home seemed, at best, hopelessly outdated. The once-laudable notion of helping worthy widows had resulted in a system that seemed to reward single motherhood over marriage and staying at home over working. What had started as an attempt to ennoble poor mothers resulted, several generations and program changes later, in stigmatizing them.

The Progressive Era resulted in two important developments. The first was state rather than local control over welfare, starting with regulation of local institutions including poorhouses, mental institutions, and hospitals. The second development was an outgrowth of the first. States, in taking control of welfare, decided to create mothers' pensions, which for the first time, directed aid at single-parent families (although only at morally fit versions of these families). Mothers' pensions were an attempt to take the stigma out of poverty assistance. Rather than punishing individuals in poverty, states began to reward motherhood, particularly in the case of widowed mothers. Mothers' aid "not only asserted a public responsibility for the poor, but also sought to remove relief from the stigma of pauperism and the poorhouse."[41] Mothers' pensions, which emphasized the dependence of mothers (on either a breadwinning spouse or the state), formed the basis of the national family welfare policy created during the New Deal.

Welfare As We Knew It

The New Deal Brings the Federal Government into the Welfare System

From the colonial period through the progressive period, providing for the poor was a function of local government in combination with private charity. Progressivism brought state governments into the welfare arena, in the provision of mothers' pensions and in regulation of institutions. It wasn't until the 1930s that the federal government got involved in welfare and then only because of an enormous economic crisis.

In 1929, the United States stock market crashed, marking the end of the rapid economic expansion of the roaring twenties and causing monetary panic throughout the United States. Between thirteen and fifteen million workers lost jobs.[42] One result of this panic was a "run" on financial institutions. Individuals, afraid that their money wasn't safe, ran to their banks and savings and loans to take out their money before the financial institutions went bankrupt. Of course, a run on a bank could cause the bank to deplete its money supplies and go out of business, since the bank didn't actually hold cash reserves for every account, but rather invested its money. In the movie *It's a Wonderful Life*, there is a scene in which there is a "run" on the Bailey Brothers' Building and Loan. George Bailey, played by Jimmy Stewart, tried to explain to his customers that they couldn't all withdraw their money at once because the building and loan didn't have sufficient cash reserves.

> You're thinking of it all wrong—as if I have the money back in a safe. The money's not here. Well, your money's in Joe's house—that's right next to yours. And then the Kennedy house and Mrs. Maiklin's house and a hundred others. Why you're lending them the money to build; then they're gonna pay it back to you as best they can. Now, what are you gonna do, foreclose on them?

Fortunately for George Bailey, he was able to keep his Building and Loan afloat. Not all financial institutions were so fortunate. One result of the Great Depression was the FDIC, the Federal Deposit Insurance Corporation, which insures the money put into a financial institution.

The depression extended far beyond the financial world, as people lost jobs and had very little income to spend on even the most basic necessities. The loss of income had a spiral effect: the less money people spent, the fewer products that stores could sell. Stores went out of business, putting their own employees out of work and further depleting the amount of spending money in the economy. Producers of goods also suffered, and factories that couldn't sell their goods had to close down, forcing their workers into unemployment. One result of the depression was deflation—a reduction in the cost of goods. From 1929 to 1933, unemployment rose from 3.2 percent to 24.9 percent. Consumption went down by 18 percent, and investment went down by 98 percent.[43] The depression was characterized not only by bank runs, but also by soup and bread lines as people on limited incomes queued up for limited resources.

As individuals experienced the devastating effects of the depression, they reached out for help. Imagine that you are an unemployed worker suffering during the depression. Where would you turn? Probably to your family first. Could they help? Most likely not. Family members wouldn't have enough money to care for themselves, much less help you out. Your next option might be private or religious charitable organizations. But private charities were faced with massive numbers of individuals requesting assistance at the same time that they saw a decrease in the amount of donations (with more and more people entering poverty, fewer and fewer people would have money to donate to charity). If family and private charity couldn't help, then perhaps local government could. Again, local government received many more applications for assistance than they could handle, and like private charities, their income was also dwindling. (The less money people earn, the less they pay in

The New Hope Mission, New York City. Photo courtesy of Corbis-Bettmann.

Hunger marchers during the depression. Photo courtesy of the Library of Congress.

taxes.) State government would be in much the same predicament. Thus, the provider of last resort would have to be the federal government. As the depression persisted, individuals, localities, and states appealed to the federal government for help. But help was not quick in coming.

Herbert Hoover, president at the start of the depression, believed that government, especially federal government, should have a very limited role in providing welfare. Speaking before the depression, Hoover stressed the role of personal responsibility.

> It is the failure of groups to respond to their responsibilities to others that drives government more and more into the lives of our people. And every time government is forced to act, we lose something in self-reliance, character, and initiative. Every time we find solutions outside of government we have not only strengthened character but we have preserved our sense of real self-government.[44]

Interestingly, this quote sounds vaguely familiar. In fact, it sounds almost like something that a politician might say today. Unfortunately for Herbert Hoover, his self-help philosophy did not fit the times.[45] When he would have preferred personal responsibility, citizens were begging for government assistance. The public began to think that he did not understand the magnitude of the crisis on individuals' lives. Hoover, who had claimed responsibility for the economic success of the 1920s, now was given the blame for the economic catastrophe of the depression. People made homeless by the depression set up encampments on the outskirts of towns, which became known as **Hoovervilles**. Hoover's Reconstruction Finance Corporation (RFC) established a relationship between government, banks, and big business, causing the public to believe he cared more for business than for the individuals affected by the depression. Will Rogers derided the RFC, saying that Hoover displayed a "trickle down" approach to solving the problem. (The same derisive terminology was later applied to supply-side economics under President Reagan.)

The real reason for Hoover's unpopularity was not so much in his policies but in his attitudes. Whereas New York Governor Franklin Delano Roosevelt, his Democratic opponent, exuded positive energy, Hoover displayed a glumness and morosity that betrayed his underlying deep concern about the problems of the depression and his diligence in trying to solve them.

> No President ever worked harder in the White House than Herbert Hoover, but he was never able to convince the nation that he cared deeply about how people were suffering and that he shared with them the sorrows and the blighted prospects depression had brought.[46]

During the presidential campaign, both candidates advocated a limited governmental role in ending the depression. Historians have struggled to find foreshadowing of the specific programs of the New Deal in Roosevelt's campaign utterances and often have come up empty-handed. Roosevelt did not

FDR signs the Social Security bill. Photo courtesy of Corbis-Bettmann.

propose during the campaign many of the programs that were to become synonymous with the New Deal, in part because he didn't want to stir up controversy prior to the election and in part because he had not yet completely formulated his ideas for the new programs. In fact, many of Roosevelt's speeches lay the blame of the depression on excess governmental spending, and he even pledged to reduce federal expenditures in at least one speech, although in others he pledged to do whatever was necessary—including federal spending—to alleviate destitution.[47] What Roosevelt did offer to the American public was energy and optimism, and that is exactly what the public wanted.

Roosevelt won the 1932 election in a landslide, and his immediate response upon taking office was action against the depression. It was in his first inaugural address that the president uttered his famous words "the only thing we have to fear is fear itself." In the first 100 days of his administration, Roosevelt pushed a variety of legislative initiatives through Congress, including a bank holiday, the end of prohibition, aid to farmers, unemployment compensation, federal regulation of the stock market, and large-scale public works programs.[48]

The centerpiece of the social welfare system that was set up by the New Deal was the **Social Security Act (SSA)** of 1935. It provided, first, for old-age pensions, and second, cash assistance for children in families without a breadwinner. Aid to Dependent Children (ADC, which later became Aid to Families with Dependent Children, and, more recently, TANF), established by the act, gave cash grants to families with minor children and no father.

The most popular part of the SSA was the social insurance program for the elderly, Old Age Insurance (OAI), which we now refer to as "social security." In the 1930s, as today, the elderly were a powerful voting bloc. In fact, Dr. Francis Everett Townsend started a movement that swept across the country, supporting a government pension of $200 per month for all retired people over the age of 60. Although the plan was voted down in Congress (by voice vote, so representatives would not have to go on record with their opposition), the force of the "Townsendites" assured members of Congress that assistance to the elderly was politically important.[49] Assistance to the aged was more generous than ADC in part because Congress was reacting to the supporters of the Townsend plan.[50] In addition, OAI had more clout because it was a federal program, provided entirely by the national government. ADC, on the other hand, was a federal-state program. States had the option to take federal money for ADC; if they chose to do so, they were expected to provide a certain amount of money themselves for the program. ADC was never as popular as social security and was given less money and less emphasis in the early years of the implementation of the Social Security Act. "Unlike the aged, children did not vote, held no property, and made but trifling purchases. Children could not, on their own, form a powerful competing constituency."[51]

ADC gave federal grants to states for what they had been doing already—providing relief to poor families through mothers' pension programs. The architects of the New Deal initially expected widows to be the recipients of ADC, as noted previously, and the program was based on the mothers' pensions programs which most states already had. Therefore, in order to be eligible for ADC, families had to have only one parent present, and that parent's income from work had to be low enough to be considered poor. The issue of single motherhood was addressed in policy debates over ADC. Federal officials thought aid should go to all families with children, including those who had no father due to desertion or illegitimate childbirth. States wanted only "nice" families (i.e., ones that didn't include a divorced or "deserted" woman) to receive aid, since that's what they were used to under mothers' pensions.[52]

The New Deal created a system of "relief" from the ravages of the depression. (At the time, "relief" was used in the same way we might talk about public assistance or welfare.) This relief was of four major types, which still exist today: general relief, work relief, categorical assistance, and social insurance.[53]

1. *General relief* was assistance given to individuals who were not able to work. Roosevelt expected that these "unemployables" would be taken care of

by the states. Today, general relief (also known as General Assistance) is provided by some states for populations not covered under federal programs. Most of the people receiving general relief have been single men, since women and their families were generally covered by AFDC.

2. *Work relief* was provided by programs such as the Works Progress Administration (WPA), the Civilian Conservation Corps (CCC), and the Tennessee Valley Authority (TVA). The federal government funded work relief programs, which gave government jobs to the unemployed. Most of the jobs were for public works such as building dams or roads. The work relief of the 1930s is similar to the idea of "workfare" today. Workfare gives jobs to people who request public assistance, giving them employment in exchange for cash grants. The work relief programs of the 1930s were of limited duration and were attacked for creating "make-work" jobs.

3. *Categorical assistance* is aid given to individuals who fall into certain categories that are deemed eligible for assistance. These categories include poor families with dependent children, the blind, and the aged. Individuals in these categories must fall under a specified income level. By far the largest category under categorical assistance is families with children. President Roosevelt intended that the federal government would provide categorical assistance to the states. States could choose whether or not to participate in the programs, but if they did, the states would have to pay a certain percentage of the costs (this is called "matching" the federal grant). Categorical assistance is still handled in much the same way today.

4. *Social insurance programs* were also funded by the federal government, paid for by an earmarked tax. Social security and unemployment compensation are social insurance programs. These programs were far less controversial than the categorical programs, since individuals receiving benefits had paid taxes for them, leading to the perception that these benefits were "earned" whereas categorical assistance was not.

Of the four types of relief, categorical programs proved the most controversial, whereas social insurance programs became the most popular. Social insurance programs are aimed at groups who society believes have earned their benefits. Categorical programs, unlike social insurance programs, are not paid for by earmarked taxes and are not based on prior work. If a single mother with children fell under the poverty line, she was eligible for ADC, even if she had never worked or paid taxes. The popular perception has been that social insurance pays people for working, whereas categorical programs pay people for not working.[54]

The New Deal marked the beginning of a new era in American welfare politics. First, it marked the beginning of federal involvement in what had once been a state and local function. Even though President Roosevelt expected to eventually give welfare back to the states, the New Deal was a centripetal force that proved difficult to counteract. Second, the New Deal had as its theoretical base the idea that poverty was a structural problem, rather than a personal one. Because of the broad and devastating effects of the depression, this idea was popularly accepted, even though at other times in our history, our philosophical bent toward individualism has interpreted poverty as a problem of individual responsibility. Third, the New Deal established a state-federal partnership in the provision of welfare services, creating the system of federal grants that became entrenched during the Great Society and War on Poverty. Fourth, the New Deal separated public assistance from social insurance, leaving room for the old distinction between worthy and unworthy poor to grow. Public assistance programs came to be viewed as charity given to people who didn't really deserve it, whereas social insurance programs were viewed as earned privileges. The distinction between the two created a stigma for AFDC and its recipients, a stigma that still exists today and that has never been applied to social security recipients.

The contrast between worthy and unworthy poor was manifest in the derisive term "the dole." Those individuals who accepted poverty assistance from the government were said to be on the dole, taking handouts rather than working for their living. And shortly after the new programs were implemented, government officials and the general public expressed fears that individuals who accepted relief might become dependent on government programs; that is, they would become so accustomed to receiving government aid that they would soon be unable to support themselves by working. In particular, the public was concerned about work relief programs, which were supposed to be only a short-term solution to the depression. Even Roosevelt, the liberal president who created the American version of the welfare state, expressed this view.

> Continued dependence upon relief induces a spiritual and moral disintegration fundamentally destructive to the national fibre. To dole out relief in this way is to administer a narcotic, a subtle destroyer of the human spirit. [The federal government] must and shall quit this business of relief.[55]

Roosevelt seemed to be of two minds about problems in the system of relief. On the one hand, he specifically criticized welfare dependence, implying that poverty is primarily an individual problem; on the other hand, his vision of government rested on the belief that society had an obligation to care for the least well-off of its citizens.

As president, Roosevelt acted on the same ideas that had guided his actions as governor—the belief that mankind had a responsibility for the well-being of all human beings, that an impersonal and uncontrolled economic system, not the unemployed themselves, usually caused unemployment, that public assistance was not a matter of charity but a matter of justice that rested upon the individual's right to a minimum standard of living in a civilized society, and that liberty and security were synonymous; thus the very existence of a democratic state depended on the health and welfare of its citizens.[56]

Despite these beliefs, Roosevelt fell short of creating a welfare state, at least in terms of the European model.[57] Public assistance was conditioned on behavior and tied to work. Welfare mothers were expected to be "morally fit"; the unemployed and the elderly were assumed to deserve assistance based on their prior work activities.

Early Criticisms of the Federal Welfare System

The welfare system of the 1930s was soon under attack, and the attacks were usually based on the idea that welfare was eroding individualism and personal responsibility. The programs that were most disliked were the temporary relief programs, which seemed to be going to the undeserving poor.

> By the late 1930s, popular attitudes seemed harsher. Reflecting this hardening, Congress regularly cut relief appropriations proposed by the administration. Majorities in polls said that most poor people could get off relief if they tried hard enough. Respondents began to distinguish between the unemployed—perhaps deserving—and "reliefers," "good-for-nothing loafers," and "pampered poverty rats" who were just as reprehensible as "paupers" had been.[58]

In 1939, the Social Security Act was amended in ways that had a profound impact on ADC. Initially, social security (retirement) benefits were to go only to workers in certain professions named in the act (for example, personal service, casual, and agriculture jobs were not covered, effectively excluding working women and minorities from social security). The benefits did not originally extend to the worker's family. The 1939 amendments expanded benefits to make the male breadwinner's family eligible for social security, including his wife, or, in the case of his death, his widow and surviving dependents. Whereas women had been excluded because of the gendered nature of the covered occupations in the original act, the 1939 amendments specifically made dependent wives eligible and married women workers (and their dependent husbands) ineligible for social security. The amendments also took most widows out of ADC and brought them into the more socially acceptable social insurance policy. Women were still treated as dependents; their eligibility for social security in most cases derived from their status as married women or widows. ADC now consisted almost entirely of divorced, "deserted," and never-married mothers. It also included the widows of men whose jobs were excluded under the act. The 1939 amendments created a two-tiered system of welfare. Worthy widows (defined by their husbands' occupations), and their families were covered by social security; other single mothers (very often minorities) received ADC.[59] ADC now quite obviously was the vehicle for the unworthy poor to receive benefits.

Not surprisingly, the unworthy poor on ADC were the subject of attacks in the media throughout the 1940s and 1950s, when "'welfare boom' stories zeroed in on chiselers and cheats, runaway husbands, live-in boyfriends, unmarried baby breeders, loafers, and drunks."[60] The 1950s saw increased attempts to make sure that these unworthy poor were removed from the welfare rolls. Money was to go only to families that had no other means of support.[61] As ADC came to be equated with immorality, particularly immorality as identified with the presence of so many illegitimate children in the caseload, many states adopted various restrictive rules under the rubric known as a "suitable home."[62] "Suitable home" provisions prohibited the single mothers receiving ADC from living with men who were not their husbands. (If the women married, they were no longer eligible for ADC.) State public officials actually raided recipients' homes in the wee hours of the morning to make sure that there was no "man in the house" whose presence would make the mother ineligible for benefits. To make matters worse, these suitable home provisions were often aimed at black women, who were more likely to have children out of wedlock. While states defended their suitable home provisions on the grounds that aid should be reserved only for those families who lived up to community standards, opponents charged that poor women in general and black women in particular were being singled out unfairly.

From early on, ADC evoked unfair criticism for encouraging undesirable social behavior. Social security provided for retired male workers, their families, and their widows; ADC went to other single-parent families who were seen as less deserving of assistance. There was no policy in place for working poor families, who were supposed to be able to take care of themselves. If, for example, ADC had been directed at children in poor families, including two-parent families, then the program could not be faulted for encouraging immoral behavior. But the program wasn't directed at two-parent families because the father was supposed to be working. ADC was stuck in a catch-22: Giving aid to single mothers opened the program to criticism for discouraging marriage and encouraging desertion, whereas giving aid to two-parent families would have opened the program to criticism for discouraging work.

The Consolidation of Welfare: The Great Society and the War on Poverty

The welfare system originated in an economic crisis. Individuals and states, unable to find relief anywhere else during the depression, turned to the federal government. The need for federal action was acute since the economic situation was bad, and the poor were so visible. The next great expansion of the welfare system came about in a very different period: one of sustained economic growth. From World War II until the 1960s, the economy was experiencing a boom. Unemployment was low (although it began to rise in the 1970s), production was high, and the consumer culture was born. Why would policymakers decide to focus on poverty in such a period? One answer was that they had the luxury to do so. Another is that poverty, which had always existed in American society, seemed particularly troublesome in a time when most Americans were reaping the benefits of rapid social and economic advances. Indeed, many of the people who lived in neatly manicured suburban areas, had radio and even television, and parked new cars in their driveways or garages in the mid-1950s were the children and grandchildren of the impoverished immigrant populations from the turn of the century.

In a society where it seemed easy to achieve the American dream, many well-to-do Americans began to feel guilty about the poverty population that would not go away. Popular books in the 1950s and 1960s included economist John Kenneth Galbraith's *The Affluent Society,* in which he lamented the poverty that existed in a wealthy nation. Socialist Michael Harrington's *The Other America* told the tale of poverty in America, describing destitute families living in shacks without running water, utterly lacking the hopes and dreams that motivated their suburban counterparts.[63] One phrase characterized the time period: "poverty amidst plenty." Americans couldn't believe that abject poverty could exist in an economy and culture as advanced and sophisticated as their own. As one policymaker put it,

> During the past twenty-five years the extent of low incomes in the United States has been diminished considerably. The social and economic reforms such as social insurance, public assistance, and minimum wage enacted in the New Deal era

and the high rate of economic growth during the 1940s and early 1950s have played important roles in the reduction of poverty.

Yet in the midst of our affluent society, millions of Americans still live in poverty. . . . What is needed is a broadscale attack on poverty and its causes from many different directions. Such an attack should include a broad program of education; income maintenance to meet basic needs; expanded health and housing programs and other services to improve the physical and social environment; an equitable and efficient tax system; and a constant effort to achieve and maintain optimum use of manpower.[64]

The concern about poverty amidst plenty first arose with respect to the poor white population, particularly in the Appalachian Mountain region. (The Appalachian Mountains extend from Alabama to Vermont and have historically housed pockets of poverty.) In 1959, the Kennedy campaign focused on poverty, unemployment, hunger, and reaction against the complacency of the 1950s as major themes. When President Johnson assumed office on Kennedy's death, one of the first things he did was to declare a **War on Poverty**, based on the results of a poverty task force commissioned by President Kennedy. President Johnson wanted to create a "**Great Society**" in which poverty was a thing of the past. Advisors, policymakers, and social thinkers climbed on the bandwagon in one of the most idealistic time periods of our country's history. Unfortunately, as bold as the poverty warriors' plan was, to eliminate poverty altogether is a goal that has never been realized. What Johnson ultimately did was to set himself up for failure.

But Johnson could not be deterred. He took on not only the rural poor whose plight had so affected the Kennedys, but also aimed his policies at urban blacks, who had experienced some success in the civil rights movement and were now ready for more broad-based reform. Johnson's reforms had as their basis the goal of rehabilitation. The idea was to change the culture of poverty by giving the poor marketable skills and otherwise empowering them to take charge of their lives. Government assistance would not simply help those in poverty, it would transform them. "The war on poverty was indeed more ambitious in its long-range goals, and therefore more intrusive and paternalistic than New Deal programs."[65]

The Great Society expanded on what the New Deal had done, further enlarging the role of the federal government in the welfare system. Johnson used categorical grants to send funds directly to cities, causing states to complain that he was bypassing them and upsetting the federal system. The federal programs of the Great Society did not stop at cities. In many instances, grants went to private or nonprofit local organizations. Community involvement was encouraged at all levels, and many programs required that boards be set up containing not only local officials but also members of the population that was to be served.

Johnson's War on Poverty, more ideological than Roosevelt's New Deal, was less popular, even at the beginning. States and localities resented further federal intrusion on their turf, and the public, having become wary of big government (the anticommunist period beginning in the 1940s had led many Americans to be fearful of "socialistic" government programs[66]), was not pleased with the layers of bureaucracy created by the War on Poverty and with the massive government spending that seemed to lack accountability. Many individuals who opposed the Great Society did so based on ideological differences of opinion as to what the proper role of government should be in solving what was probably an insoluble problem and as to what level of government should ultimately be responsible for poverty programs. Others opposed the new programs for reasons that had to do with race, since many of the new federal programs were targeted at the urban black population. As much as the poverty warriors may have wanted to help this population, they sowed the seeds of resentment: Working-class whites began to feel under siege. Why should their hard-earned tax dollars go to pay for programs that they believed excluded them?

Programs under the War on Poverty included Comprehensive Employment and Training Act (CETA), new-towns-in-town, public housing, expansion of welfare benefits, OEO, affirmative action, Head Start, Upward Bound, Neighborhood Youth Corp., Job Corps, and Legal Services. The counterpart to the New Deal's Social Security Act of 1935 was the **Economic Opportunity Act of 1964**, which established the Office of Economic Opportunity (OEO) and created community action agencies, local organizations that were to become the recipients of the federal grants from the OEO.[67] The OEO programs were based on a popular idea of the time—that there was a "culture of poverty" that prevented poor people from developing the skills, attitudes, and outlooks that were necessary to succeed in American society. So far this sounds like the theory behind the 1996 welfare reform bill. However, in the "culture of poverty" view of the 1960s, the poor were not to be held responsible for their own condition, but rather could be helped to overcome it. The culture of poverty was based on structural problems in the economy and society. OEO programs tried to do more than remold the poor into the ideal of the middle class, as the progressives and poorhouse advocates had tried to do earlier; OEO programs "empowered" the poor, giving them political as well as cultural tools to deal with society.[68]

Policymakers of the Great Society were aware that many of the poor—especially in the South—faced more than economic and social barriers. Blacks in the urban North and rural South faced racial barriers to advancement. The

LBJ signs the "War on Poverty" bill. Photo courtesy of Corbis-Bettmann.

civil rights movement worked to desegregate educational and other public fa-
cilities; War on Poverty programs attempted to make up for past discrimination by directing aid to the minorities who had been the subject of discrimination for decades. Because local officials in the South had been responsible for
much of the discrimination, policymakers created community action agencies
to administer the new programs. However noble the attempt might have been,
the community action agencies created resentment among local authorities,
who felt that power was being wrongfully taken from them. Remember that
social policy had been primarily a local function right up to the New Deal.
Even New Deal programs maintained some semblance of local control. Great
Society programs, on the other hand, specifically took control away from the
local government, putting it instead into the hands of the local community action agencies, which were to be racially mixed and include members of the target population.

   LBJ defended his attempts at bypassing local governments as "creative federalism," which he believed was a necessary response to the unwillingness and

inability of state and local governments, particularly in the South, to act on social policy and civil rights issues. Creative federalism attempted to control state
and local governments not only through community action agencies, but also
by requiring affirmative action and citizen participation as a condition of federal aid.[69] The method of control—community action agencies—was being
used for arguably good purposes—reducing discrimination. On the other
hand, localities could also argue that they had a right to control local programs. The dispute became bitter, especially with the issue of race involved.
Anyone who argued for local or state control was immediately suspect as a
racist; the old "states' rights" argument had served to defend institutionalized
racism since the Civil War.

The War on Poverty probably went too far—inasmuch as it imposed directed federal resources in a way that interfered with local governments in a
nation that valued local community and individualism. The War on Poverty
tried to encourage a sense of community, but in creating federal programs implemented at the local level, it set itself up for the charge that one policy or
program couldn't possibly work in every city or town in the United States.
"Johnson's uplifting vision of the Great Society was a call for energetic federal
action in the confident belief that such a decisive tilt toward federal power con-
stituted no threat to the American democratic system."[70]

One of the dominant themes of the War on Poverty was the notion of *opportunity*. The poor were not so because of moral failings or lack of character;
they were poor because they did not have the same opportunities that middle-
class Americans had. Buoyed by the successes of the civil rights movement, the
poverty warriors optimistically believed that they could change people's lives
by giving them opportunities: to get jobs, to gain skills, to go to school, to edu-
cate their children. The War on Poverty rested on the belief that government
could help people to help themselves and that, in so doing, we could create a
better society. Community action agencies and other local initiatives not only
helped the poor; they also created a more democratic society where individuals participated in local government and local programs (even though those
programs were funded at the national level). Redistributing income to the
poor was a way not only to create more opportunities, but also a way to make
society more equitable and thus more democratic.

The Great Society impacted public assistance for women and children.
ADC, which had been renamed Aid to Families with Dependent Children
(AFDC) in 1950, began to actively encourage work as part of the new emphasis
on rehabilitation.[71] The Work Incentive Program (WIN), established in 1967,
provided job preparation activities for welfare recipients and made federal

funding available to states that wished to develop demonstration programs to encourage work.[72] Organizations such as the National Welfare Rights Organization (NWRO) sought to bring FDR's ideas to their full fruition: that poverty is not an individual but rather a structural problem, that the government has an obligation to help the poor, that the poor have a right to this assistance, which is not to be considered charity. This view of community emphasized societal obligation rather than personal responsibility, since society, rather than the poor themselves, was responsible for poverty. Combined with the civil rights movement, the War on Poverty raised the poor's expectations about what the government could and should do for them.[73] At the time of the New Deal, the poor were accustomed to working hard with little hope of getting ahead and to limited assistance from the government. They were reluctant to go "on the dole." By the 1960s, the poor had become more expectant, more organized, and more demanding of their rights.[74]

One of the main differences between the War on Poverty and the New Deal was that President Johnson was attempting to eradicate poverty during an economic boom, whereas many of President Roosevelt's programs were temporary solutions to a temporary crisis.[75] Although social insurance was a long-term policy, it was acceptable because it was tied to work and because large numbers of middle-class Americans were made eligible for it. The War on Poverty had as its premise a structuralist interpretation: The capitalistic economy left behind a certain number of people and economic growth could not bring everyone out of poverty. Rehabilitating the poor and providing them with economic opportunities became societal goals.

Was the Great Society successful? The answer, of course, depends on how you look at it. Obviously, poverty was not eliminated entirely. Defenders of the Great Society say that it did help alleviate poverty, reduce racial discrimination, and chip away at the stigma attached to being poor. It also helped to equalize the treatment of the poor throughout the United States by creating national programs with minimum standards. They also contend that although some of the programs didn't work as intended, others were never fully tested. By the late 1960s, Johnson's attention was diverted from the War on Poverty to the Vietnam War, and funding and implementation of Great Society programs were put on the back burner. Opponents of the Great Society claim that it did nothing more than coddle the poor and create a population that expected entitlements from the government and in fact became dependent on those entitlements. Worse still, they believe, it introduced perverse incentives that encouraged the breakup of families, out-of-wedlock births, and the intrusion of a bloated federal bureaucracy in what should have been state and local activities.

Ending Welfare As We Knew It

Resentment of federal intrusion into state activities resulted in a radical proposal to both deal with poverty and reduce the federal bureaucracy. The proposed program, called the Family Assistance Plan (FAP), would have created a guaranteed minimum annual income for families. If a family made less than an established amount, it would note it on its tax return, and the government would make up the difference in what is called a negative income tax. If a family made more than this amount, it would be taxed as usual. FAP would have eliminated AFDC entirely, getting rid of eligibility forms and paperwork, although it would have instituted work requirements. Welfare would no longer exist since every family had a right to a minimum income that was guaranteed by the government. That this idea—which sounds more socialistic than capitalistic—was proposed in the United States was surprising. The politician who proposed it, even more surprisingly, was President Richard M. Nixon.

Why on earth would a Republican propose such a program? There were several reasons. First, economists (even conservative economists) of the time felt it was the only way to eliminate the work disincentive inherent in welfare (that a person can often make more money by staying on welfare than by working).[76] Second, whereas liberals were intent on rehabilitation (providing services such as education and job training to welfare recipients to help them overcome the barriers that kept them in poverty), the conservative reaction was that the poor didn't need government services (which cost a lot of money); they needed cash to get them out of poverty. Conservatives argued that the minimum income would provide cash and reward work. (FAP required adults to participate in work or training, or lose benefits.[77]) Also, Nixon's FAP was part of his strategy to court the middle class, which he referred to as the "silent majority." FAP would appeal to the silent majority because it eliminated the hated welfare system and gave aid to the working poor.[78] Finally, the Family Assistance Plan would eliminate the welfare bureaucracy that had been set up by the War on Poverty. Social workers also happened to be representatives of Democratic programs in inner cities. Getting rid of them would also get rid of Democratic pork barrel.

Nixon sent his FAP proposal to Congress, offering three main arguments in support of it: (1) the welfare system as currently constructed discouraged work; (2) cash grants put more money in the hands of the poor than do government services; (3) the welfare system was causing the breakup of the family.[79] Nixon's proposal failed in Congress. Opposition came from both the left and the right. Conservatives felt that it was too expensive, that it would in-

TABLE 2.1   The Evolution and Devolution of Welfare Policy

Elizabethan Poor Law 1601	Governmental obligation to assist the poor is established.
Colonial Poor Laws 1600s–1700s	Localities are in control: Community responsibility is prevalent; local governments provide assistance.
Poorhouse Era 1800s	Localities are still in control: The focus is on individualism; local government provides institutions to care for the poor.
Progressive Movement early 1900s	States begin to take over control by regulating local institutions, providing mothers' aid, workers' compensation, and unemployment insurance.
New Deal 1930s	Welfare becomes a federal-state program; government funds at the national level what the states had been doing at the local level, requires a state match.
Great Society 1960s	Within the federal program, local input is stressed. Emphasis is on community responsibility—communities run federally funded programs.
The "Waiver State" 1980s–1990s	Power devolves partially to state governments: States receive more flexibility in running federally funded programs.
Welfare as a Block Grant 1996	Power is further devolved to the states: Congress passes legislation requiring states to run welfare programs at their own discretion, using federal money with very few strings attached.

crease the welfare rolls, and that the cash would actually create a disincentive to work.[80] Liberals thought the guaranteed minimum income ($1,600) was too low, were unhappy that FAP would eliminate some of their pet programs, and thought the program demonstrated a negative attitude toward the poor.[81] In addition, Democrats did not want Nixon to get credit for reforming welfare. The National Welfare Rights Organization recruited welfare recipients to testify against the proposal,[82] which ultimately failed in Congress.

President Reagan took an entirely different approach to welfare. Although he agreed with Nixon's indictment of the welfare system as breaking up the family and discouraging work, Reagan wanted to both decrease federal spending and tie welfare benefits to behavior.[83] Where Nixon's plan had the goal of assistance at its base, Reagan was more interested in deterrence. Reagan's "turnback" proposal for welfare would have given states complete funding and administrative responsibility for AFDC. In exchange, the federal government

would have assumed the entire cost of Medicaid. The *devolution* of responsibility from national to state government would have put welfare back where it
had been before the Great Depression. (See Table 2.1.) The Republican welfare
reform law passed in 1996 did not go nearly as far as Reagan's turnback proposal had. Although the Personal Responsibility Act cut funding for welfare
and gave administrative responsibility to the states, it did not end the federal
role in providing funds or establishing requirements, as President Reagan's
proposal would have done. Reagan's proposals for welfare were as ideologically
based as Johnson's had been, although from a polar opposite perspective. Reagan and the conservatives had three main goals in the 1980s: (1) to end the liberal ascendancy in national government; (2) to move public programs to the
private sector whenever possible; and (3) to keep entitlements limited.[84]

President Reagan's popularity with the public was due both to the force of
his personality (in this way, he was similar to President Roosevelt) and to his
ability to vocalize middle-class hostility toward a government that seemed to
be spending money on programs that they felt rewarded negative behavior.

> The economic hardships of the 1980s and 1990s have spawned a resentment of
> entitlements. Millions of people working hard to survive and provide for their
> children resent the bite of taxes, especially tax money they believe to be benefiting
> others, who, they imagine, may not be working as hard. "Entitlements" has be-
> come a code word for undeserved benefits.[85]

Whereas the Great Society created programs to rehabilitate the poor, the
Reagan Revolution sought to reduce dependency on those programs. Whereas
the Great Society expanded the role of the federal government in providing
welfare under "creative federalism," the Reagan Revolution sought to give authority back to the states under "new federalism." The Reagan administration
cut welfare benefits to people already on the rolls, restricted eligibility for programs, attempted to give more responsibility for social programs to the states,
and used welfare for *deterrence*—making welfare undesirable.

> When Ronald Reagan was elected president, he promised to roll back the welfare
> state. His 1981 Omnibus Budget Reconciliation Act [OBRA] eliminated the entire
> public service jobs program, removed 400,000 individuals from the food stamp
> program, and reduced or eliminated welfare and Medicaid benefits for the work-
> ing poor.[86]

Although his devolution never occurred, Reagan was able to cut spending on
government social programs, and he encouraged state experimentation on
welfare by cutting spending on WIN and allowing states to apply for waivers
from welfare requirements in order to create innovative programs.

Despite the fact that Reagan proposed eliminating the welfare system entirely, he ended up signing a centrist welfare reform bill in 1988. The **Family Support Act** was based on a new consensus between liberals and conservatives. Liberals conceded that conservatives were right in their assumption that work helps welfare recipients; conservatives conceded that welfare recipients need services such as child care and medical care in order to work.

> At the heart of the Family Support Act (FSA) is the concept of reciprocity, the expectation that a standard of conduct would be a condition for receipt of welfare. The conservative idea of reciprocity meant that AFDC recipients would be expected to work or engage in job training in order to obtain benefits.[87]

Although Reagan's turnback proposal had been more conservative than the 1996 PRWORA, the bill he ultimately signed was much more liberal. Interestingly, the FSA was negotiated and advocated in Congress by the head of the National Governors' Association (NGA), then governor Bill Clinton of Arkansas. In the 1988 welfare reform debate, Senator Daniel Patrick Moynihan (D–NY) was to the right of center: He proposed welfare reform that was closer to the Reagan administration proposal than to Democratic proposals in Congress. In 1996 he was considered far to the left in his defense of welfare as an entitlement. The Family Support Act instituted an employment and training program called JOBS (for Job Opportunities and Basic Skills) which included federal funds for child care for program participants. The FSA also instituted mandatory work requirements, strengthened child support enforcement provisions (which strictly enforce an absent parent's obligation to make payments to support his children), and established transitional child care and Medicaid benefits to help persons leaving AFDC for employment.

One of the signs that the FSA was a moderate bill was that both liberals and conservatives were not entirely satisfied with it. Liberal groups complained that the bill did not create a minimum national benefit and conservatives felt its work requirements were not strict enough. The FSA was remarkable in that it was the result of a compromise between welfare advocates and Republicans in Congress—something that had not been thought possible. The time appeared right for a "new consensus."

> Although many actors were involved in welfare reform consideration, the key factor may have been what Senator Moynihan called "syzygy," in astronomy, a rare alignment of the earth, moon, and sun, or in this case, a new consensus among liberals and conservatives that welfare recipients should both be required to be involved in some type of employment activity and be given some level of supportive services (such as child care) to assist in their participation in work and training programs.[88]

The JOBS program was expected to greatly reduce the number of people on welfare and to encourage work among welfare recipients. Unfortunately, the program never lived up to its expectations. In part, this was because the economy experienced a downturn just as JOBS was being implemented. Also, the program oversold itself. Thus, although JOBS had been billed as a major overhaul of welfare, one that reflected a new consensus among liberals and conservatives, welfare was still a viable political issue. In his 1992 presidential campaign, Arkansas Governor Bill Clinton, an architect of the Family Support Act, pledged to "end welfare as we know it." Once in office, President Clinton's first attempt at major social legislation was not in welfare but in health care. His initiative failed, paving the way for the election of a Republican Congress in 1994 and severely curtailing his ability to take the lead in welfare reform.

With the passage of the Personal Responsibility and Work Opportunity Reconciliation Act of 1996 (discussed in detail in the later chapters), welfare has moved from a New Deal and Great Society program to one based on Republican ideology. Whereas the first half of this century saw the evolution of welfare to a national-state and national-local function, the past couple of decades have ushered in a devolution of federal authority. State responsibility has been greatly increased under the PRWORA, something that conservatives have been arguing for since the New Deal. Spending has been decreased, and welfare focuses on the twin goals of deterrence and rehabilitation. The PRWORA is the most sweeping revision of welfare law in this country since the passage of the Social Security Act of 1935. It marks a high point in the recent Republican attempts to dismantle the New Deal and Great Society and establishes conservative hegemony in social welfare policy. It also shifts responsibility for the problems of welfare squarely onto the shoulders of the states and of the Republican architects of the plan. Liberals claim that welfare will not only continue to be a problem, but that cuts in welfare will send huge numbers of families into poverty over the next several years. If the PRWORA is successful, Republicans will be able to take credit for having solved the welfare mess. If it is not, they will have to take at least part of the blame.

Conclusion

There is more continuity in the history of welfare in the United States than one might expect. One common theme has been the distinction between the truly needy, who deserve societal assistance, and the able-bodied poor, whom society views as undeserving of government help. At various times in our history, we have paid more attention to assisting the truly needy; at other times, we have focused our efforts on deterring the able-bodied poor from receiving government aid. The New Deal was a popular attempt at assisting the poor, since an economic crisis had caused large numbers of people to fall into poverty. This economic crisis enabled the country to view poverty as a structural rather than an individual problem—a view that historically has had limited popularity in the United States. Our faith in the capitalistic system, combined with our confidence in the Protestant work ethic, leads Americans to believe that anyone can succeed through hard work and perseverance. Thus, Americans often view welfare with suspicion since it has the potential to discourage individual responsibility and encourage dependence on governmental assistance. The American dilemma of welfare has long revolved around the question of how to help those who are in need of assistance without creating dependence among those who are capable of working. Social security and unemployment insurance are acceptable government programs since they provide assistance to the elderly and to those who have participated in the workforce. Assistance to poor families is more problematic, not only because the parents in those families are generally capable of work, but also because the program requirements focus attention on morality, particularly out-of-wedlock births. Although there are many who believe that poverty always has been and always will be a structural problem—an artifact of our capitalistic system—there are others who believe that it is primarily an individual problem. Americans have a long history of helping the poor and just as long a history of trying to ensure that those who receive our help are deserving of it.

3

....

Welfare Reform in the Policymaking Process

Legislation unquestionably generates legislation. Every statute may be said to have a long lineage of statutes behind it; and whether that lineage may be honorable or of ill repute is as much a question as to each individual statute as it can be with regard to the ancestry of each individual legislator. Every statute in its turn has a numerous progeny, and only time and opportunity can decide whether its offspring will bring it honor or shame. Once begin the dance of legislation, and you must struggle through its mazes as best you can to its breathless end—if any end there be.

Woodrow Wilson

W oodrow Wilson's description of the congressional process as the "dance of legislation" is an apt one. In order to become law, a bill usually must be introduced in both the House and the Senate, be considered by one or more committees in each chamber, be scheduled for floor debate and votes, and if the legislation has not been passed in identical form in both houses, it must be considered by a conference committee (made up of members of both the House and Senate) and sent back to each chamber for another vote. Even if all of this occurs, the bill still may die without becoming law if the president chooses to veto it. As complicated as the procedure sounds in this brief description, it is in actuality an even more intricate process, for politics plays an integral role in the passage of legislation. Democratic and Republican leaders often maneuver behind the scenes to make compromises or deals, and congressional leaders also negotiate with administration officials to ensure even before the bill is sent to the president that he will sign it. The legislative process is indeed like an old-fashioned dance, one that might be seen in a movie version of a Jane Austen novel. The end result might be breathtaking, but only if each individual knows his or her steps and performs them properly. If all the pieces fit together properly, legislation results. If not, the entire process must be repeated.

Wilson also says that "legislation unquestionably generates legislation." We never seem to be fully satisfied with the legislation that makes it through the complex and complicated process. Perhaps it isn't working as intended. Or perhaps society or the economy has changed, making adjustments to the legislation necessary. In any event, once Congress has passed a law in a particular area, it often revisits that law. Welfare policy, like other governmental policies, is made through a combination of consensus, compromise, and bargaining, and once one alternative has been selected, the policy process is not over. The public and the government continue to evaluate policies, even after they have been enacted. These evaluations often lead to calls for changes. Thus, the policy process is very often a circular one.

One result of the circular nature of the policy process is **incrementalism**. The evaluation stage of the process usually leads to minor changes rather than major overhauls of policy. Policies are changed incrementally, or a little bit at a time. The problem with incrementalism is that we often end up with piece-meal policies, since we rarely eliminate a program and start entirely from scratch.[1] AFDC was initially intended as a temporary program to help widows with small children. Since mothers in middle-class families generally didn't work at the time, AFDC mothers also were not expected to work. By the 1980s, most women with children worked, and there were many more divorced and never-married mothers than widows. Although policymakers tried to change AFDC to encourage work and discourage out-of-wedlock births, those changes were superimposed on the already-existing program. Policymakers did not create an entirely new program with new assumptions and philoso-phies that more accurately reflected economic and social realities. Occasion-ally, major nonincremental changes have been proposed. Nixon's Family Assis-tance Plan, which would have scrapped welfare entirely and replaced it with a guaranteed minimum income, never became law. Part of the reason for this (in addition to ideological opposition from both the right and the left) was that welfare recipients and workers in the welfare bureaucracy were reluctant to completely change a system in which they were already invested. Such aversion to change is common in any bureaucratic system, whether it is a welfare agency, defense agency, or private corporation.

In 1996, however, a major, nonincremental change in welfare law was not only proposed but enacted. The remainder of this chapter examines the dance of legislation in Congress to see just how this change came about. The change was substantial, for it involved a new solution to an old dilemma. The empha-sis would no longer be on long-term poverty assistance; rather, the new welfare law would reduce dependence by making government assistance temporary and conditional. The congressional process also leads to other dilemmas. In this case, many Democrats had to choose between their ideological position on welfare and the tide of public opinion, whereas Republicans had to choose be-tween compromising to attain reform or standing firm for political gain.

The Agenda-Setting Process for Welfare

In 1994, President Clinton introduced the Work and Responsibility Act, which was his vehicle to "end welfare as we know it." His plan had four basic tenets:

1. Make work pay;
2. Limit assistance to two years;

3. Strengthen child support enforcement;
4. Provide education, training, and supportive services.

Clinton's proposal also suggested targeting job training at teenage mothers new to AFDC.[2] Clinton's proposal reflected the "new consensus" from the Family Support Act, which, as chair of the National Governors' Association, he had helped shepherd to passage in 1988. The idea behind the FSA was that work activity should be required of welfare recipients and that the government should make work more desirable than welfare by increasing both supportive services and job skills training. What was new in Clinton's 1994 proposal was a time limit on welfare, something that was being tried in several states. The time limit—a deterrent to welfare—was supposed to act in concert with child care, job training, and an increase in the Earned Income Tax Credit (which reduces the tax burden of poor families with children), all of which would assist and rehabilitate welfare recipients. Clinton also suggested that welfare reform would eventually save money. The more welfare recipients entered the workforce, the less money would have to be spent on welfare payments. Liberals understood this to mean that money would have to be spent up front to provide the services that would encourage work.

By the time Clinton's proposal was finalized, the Republicans were about to win control of both houses in Congress. The Contract with America, which swept conservative Republicans into the House of Representatives, had as one of its planks a proposal to end welfare. The contract proposed to go several steps further than Clinton had. First, following Clinton's suggestion that welfare reform could save money, the Republicans proposed cutting spending on welfare. Second, expanding on Clinton's time limit, Republicans proposed a five-year *lifetime* limit for the receipt of welfare payments. Third, to encourage further efforts at deterring families from applying for welfare, the Republican contract offered states greater flexibility in administering welfare, giving states the option of taking welfare as a **block grant** (which generally provides fewer restrictions and less money than categorical grants). Finally, the Contract with America, following Clinton's suggestion that welfare reform could save money, proposed cutting government spending on welfare.

The Republican Congress passed welfare reform three times between 1994 and 1996. Twice President Clinton vetoed the legislation. The third time, three months before the November elections, President Clinton signed the Personal Responsibility and Work Opportunity Reconciliation Act (PRWORA). The act went much further than President Clinton's reform and was more sweeping than even the reform delineated in the Contract with America. The PRWORA

Clinton confers with Dole and Gingrich: Three
important players in the passage of welfare reform legislation in 1996. Photo courtesy of the
Library of Congress.

eliminated the AFDC program, which had been the centerpiece of welfare
since the Great Depression. In its place, it established block grants to the states
for the purpose of creating their own welfare programs. Although the states
have more flexibility, the act requires that states move welfare recipients into
work within two years of receiving welfare and establishes a five-year lifetime
limit for receipt of benefits. (There are some exceptions to these rules.) The
PRWORA also reduces federal expenditures, mostly by denying benefits to
legal immigrants (illegal immigrants have always been ineligible for benefits)
and by cutting spending on the food stamp program.

    In less than ten years, what had been a centrist position on welfare—main-
taining the entitlement status while encouraging welfare clients to work by
spending more money on supportive services and job training—had become the
far left position, at least as measured by votes in Congress. Twenty-five of forty-
six Democrats in the Senate voted for the PRWORA, and fully half of the Democrats in the House voted for it. And although President Clinton's cabinet was almost universally opposed to the welfare reform bill, the president, in a dramatic

TABLE 3.1   The Evolution of a New Democrat

- In 1988, Governor William Clinton of Arkansas negotiates a compromise between Democrats and Republicans in Congress on welfare reform. In what is hailed as a "new consensus" on welfare, congressional policymakers agree to both require work and increase spending on supportive services such as child care and transportation costs. Conservatives and liberals alike herald the new expansive welfare reform, titled the Family Support Act.
- In 1992, Governor Clinton runs for president as a "New Democrat," offering a moderate position on welfare reform. Building on the consensus established with the Family Support Act (which is now widely perceived to be insufficient to address the problems of welfare), candidate Clinton proposes to limit welfare benefits to two years (after which work is required) and increase spending on job preparation activities and supportive services.
- In 1994, President Clinton finally sends his welfare reform proposal to Congress. The proposal is basically dead on arrival due to the dramatic failure of health care policy the year before. The proposal would have increased spending on welfare by $10 billion, but it languishes in the Democratic-majority Congress.
- In 1996, after having weathered defeats on his welfare and health care policy proposals and after having twice vetoed Republican welfare reform legislation, President Clinton finally signs into law the most conservative, far-reaching welfare bill in history, giving Republicans their biggest victory in their "Contract with America." The Personal Responsibility and Work Opportunity Reconciliation Act not only decreases welfare spending by $55 billion over five years, it also ends the entitlement that the poor have historically had to welfare. It not only limits welfare recipients to two years before they must work, it also establishes a total lifetime limit of five years on welfare.

SOURCE: Jeffrey L. Katz, "Clinton's Changing Welfare Views," *Congressional Quarterly Weekly Report,* July 27, 1996, p. 2116.

shift, voted to reduce spending and end the entitlement status of a program he had, for much of his political career, sought to expand (see Table 3.1).

The obvious question is, How did this shift on welfare occur? How was the Republican majority able to get congressional Democrats and a Democratic president to acquiesce on their general principles of welfare reform? And why did Democrats, after sixty years, turn away from New Deal and Great Society goals and programs? As we shall see, the answers to those questions can be rather complicated. Welfare reform in 1996 was the result of a combination of factors, most of them having to do with politics. The fact that welfare reform was passed in a presidential election year is no coincidence. The specter of Republican attacks against Democrats as being soft on the issue was a strong incentive for Democratic congresspersons to vote for reform and for President Clinton to sign it. The fact that public opinion appeared to be strongly opposed to welfare also played a role. The weakening of the president after the failure of health care reform was an important factor, as was the weakened role of liberal interest groups, who played a much less visible role in welfare reform in 1996 than they had in any previous attempt.

To begin our journey through the policy process for welfare reform, let us turn to John Kingdon, whose book *Agendas, Alternatives, and Public Policies* outlines the way that a particular issue may come to the top of the governmental agenda. Viewed in a linear fashion, the public policy process may be said to have several steps or stages: *agenda-setting* is the stage in which policy problems are brought to the attention of governmental actors; in the *formulation* stage various solutions to the problems are formed by governmental officials, interest groups, or other actors; *legitimation* happens when one of the solutions is selected and becomes law; *implementation* occurs after the passage of legislation, when federal, state, or local agencies actually run the programs; finally, *evaluation* is the stage in which laws are analyzed to determine whether or not they are effective, have unintended consequences, or actually do what they are supposed to. The policy process does not actually work in a linear fashion, first, because evaluation often leads back to agenda-setting, and more importantly, the stages of the process may be occurring simultaneously rather than in an ordered fashion. For example, interest groups may be formulating policies for issues that are not yet on the governmental agenda. However, delineating the stages of the process provides a useful tool for analyzing the history of a particular piece of legislation. Kingdon focuses on the agenda-setting stage. In order for an issue to become part of the governmental agenda, according to Kingdon, a "policy window" must open up. This window of opportunity opens when three streams—political, policy, and problem—join together and the time is ripe for legislation to pass. The window of opportunity does not stay open long, however, and action must be taken quickly before the particular issue's time has come and gone.

The Problem Stream for Welfare Policy

In order for an issue to come to the government's attention, the government and the general public must consider it a problem. For example, years may go by without airline safety being a primary concern, but after a few major accidents, suddenly airline safety makes it to the top of the public's list of policy problems. Almost since the time of the New Deal, welfare policy has been on the governmental agenda in one way or another. Just about every president since Roosevelt has attempted some effort at reforming the welfare system (see Table 3.2). At var-

TABLE 3.2 Presidential Welfare Reform Initiatives

President	Year	Welfare Reform Activities
Franklin Delano Roosevelt (D)	1935	Signs *Social Security Act* (SSA), establishing *Aid to Dependent Children* (ADC).
	1939	Signs amendments to SSA that bring widows under social security, leaving other single mothers in the ADC program.
Harry S. Truman (D)	1950	Signs amendments changing the name of ADC to *Aid to Families with Dependent Children* (AFDC), extending aid to mothers, as well as their children.
John F. Kennedy (D)	1960	Proposes amendments extending AFDC to unemployed fathers; amendments pass Congress.
Richard Nixon (R)	1972	Proposes *Family Assistance Plan* (FAP). Would have eliminated welfare entirely, replacing it with a guaranteed minimum income. Fails in Congress.
Jimmy Carter (D)	1979	Proposes *Program for Better Jobs and Income* (PBJI). Fails in Congress.
Ronald Reagan (R)	1981	Proposes "turning back" administration and funding of welfare to states in exchange for federal control of Medicaid.
	1987	Signs *Family Support Act*, bipartisan welfare reform agreement supported by NGA.
William Clinton (D)	1994	Proposes moderate welfare reform with time limits after which recipients must work.
	1996	Signs conservative *Personal Responsibility and Work Opportunity Reconciliation Act*, ending welfare's entitlement.

ious points in time, welfare moves ahead on the government's agenda. According to Kingdon, there are three reasons for an issue becoming a problem: feedback, indicators, and crisis. Welfare had feedback and indicators, and at least the perception that it was a crisis.

Welfare did not enter the problem stream in any dramatic way in the early 1990s. Since the Family Support Act of 1988 had been a major overhaul of the entire welfare system, one could assume that another overhaul would not be necessary, at least for the short term. But, in fact, feedback from the Family Support Act indicated problems with the program. The goal of the act had been to spend more money on supportive services to put more welfare recipients into the workforce. As the act was being implemented, several problems with achieving this goal emerged. First, the economy had entered a downturn after passage of the FSA, making it difficult to meet the rosy projections the legislation had for finding jobs for welfare clients. Second, the act did not receive as much funding as its authors had envisioned, further limiting its possibility for success. And third, early results from implementation indicated that even with a strong job market, the FSA still didn't have enough teeth in it to force welfare clients to work. Combined, these three factors led to disappointing results and calls to come up with more stringent welfare reform.

Feedback also came from states, which had been implementing their own innovative forms of welfare reform. Starting with the Reagan administration, the federal government encouraged states to come up with new approaches to welfare and then apply for "**waivers**" from the rules of the AFDC program. The waivers usually required approval from the Department of Health and Human Services or other federal agencies. Presidents Bush and Clinton also were generous in granting waivers, and the result was an explosion of new state programs. Although some involved work or training programs, the vast majority created new restrictions, such as requiring teenage welfare mothers to live with their parents, cutting off benefits if a mother had additional children while on welfare, or tying receipt of benefits to school attendance or grades.

Although feedback was the primary method by which welfare reform entered the problem stream, there was also a perception of a crisis in the welfare system. This perception did not result from a specific event, but rather from a generalized feeling that welfare somehow rewarded the wrong kinds of behavior. The focus was on AFDC, which, as we saw in Chapter 2, was initially supported in the 1930s as a small program for "worthy widows" but, through a variety of changes in law and society, had evolved into an expansive program for single, never-married mothers, many of whom were the second or third generation of their families to receive AFDC. A sense of unfairness pervaded the American public: the working poor felt that welfare recipients got more benefits by not working; middle- and upper-income Americans did not like to see their tax dollars being spent on intergenerational welfare families. Lurking just beneath the surface of these resentments were the racial undertones of welfare: many people believed that most of the undeserving welfare recipients were black or minority. Finally, welfare recipients themselves began to feel resentful that they were the focus of so much anger; that senseless rules and regulations stymied their efforts to make better lives for themselves; that staying on welfare, as demeaning as it might be, was actually more economically rewarding than working, since by going to work a recipient would lose not only medical benefits but also incur day care costs.

Politicians could easily see that welfare was a lightning rod issue. With the mention of the words "welfare reform" one could stir up deep-seated anger from a variety of groups, many of whom were likely to vote. "Welfare reform" might be a code word for racial stereotyping, or for excessive government spending, or for bloated government bureaucracies, or for misguided liberal attempts to engineer society. When politicians come across an issue that can stir up so many emotions in so many people, they do not often hesitate to use it. Elected officials and people running for office added to the perception that there was a crisis in welfare by using it as a campaign issue. This is not to say that there were not real problems with welfare. Far from it. But much of the rhetoric about welfare reform in the 1990s (and historically) has served to highlight the problems and stir up resentment without outlining specific goals for reform. Thus, by the mid-1990s, welfare was a problem awaiting a solution.

The Policy Stream

In spite of all the demagoguery surrounding welfare reform, there were some solutions floating around in the policy stream. Specific policy proposals were already being tested in the states, which, by the mid-1990s, were trying out new programs under the waiver process. The states began using these policies not so much as specific proposals for federal reform, but as examples of what could be accomplished with more *flexibility*. States felt constrained by the rules of AFDC, and applying for a waiver from those rules was too unwieldy. "Give us the money," governors were saying to the federal government, "and let us design our own welfare systems."

Historically, the federal government has not been too anxious to give authority over welfare programs back to the states. Democrats in particular are concerned that the federal government not give up its obligation to the poor, an obligation dating back at least as far as the New Deal. In addition, Democrats argue, all states will not treat welfare recipients the same, thus creating inequities in the system of assistance to the poor. Finally, the federal government has more resources to spend on welfare, and if the states are using federal funds, then they should be accountable to the federal government. In recent years, Democrats have been increasingly likely to see the merits of state flexibility, and President Clinton, himself a former governor, granted more federal waivers from the rules than his predecessors. However, the original Clinton welfare plan maintained authority at the federal level.

The Clinton welfare proposal, which was submitted to Congress in June of 1994, rested on four planks: time limits after which recipients would be required to work, increased child support enforcement (requiring welfare mothers to identify the fathers of their children and then forcing those fathers to make child support payments), reducing teenage pregnancy, and assisting welfare clients in finding jobs by providing child care and other incentives to work. Clinton, anxious to portray himself as a centrist Democrat, proposed what was then considered a very moderate bill. The fact that a Democrat would propose a time limit for welfare was a shift rightward. In 1988, proposals to require welfare recipients to work in exchange for benefits (workfare) were branded "slavefare."[3] Now a Democratic president was proposing a time limit of two years before recipients were required to find jobs. Granted, they were not eliminated from the welfare rolls after two years, simply required to work, but this was still a daring move for a Democrat. In addition, the bill proposed to spend more money, not less, on welfare, on the grounds that it costs money to give welfare clients the skills and support they need to find a job.

The idea of a time limit for welfare had been brewing for several years, and in some ways it was a natural extension of the premise behind the Family Support Act. In the mid-1980s, Lawrence Mead, in his book *Beyond Entitlement*, had posited the notion that there was a two-way obligation in welfare: Not only did the government have an obligation to help the needy, but those receiving welfare had an obligation to society that could be fulfilled by gainful employment. In the 1980s and increasingly in the 1990s states had requested waivers to develop workfare programs. And Democrats as well as Republicans began to discuss the notion of limiting receipt of benefits to encourage welfare clients to find jobs. David Ellwood, a dean at Harvard's Kennedy School of Government, wrote extensively on this issue and was tapped (along with Mary Jo Bane, his colleague at the Kennedy School) to be an assistant secretary with responsibility for welfare reform in the Department of Health and Human Services. It was Ellwood and Bane who were the architects of the Clinton welfare reform legislation.

But while Democrats were moving to the right, so too were Republicans. The Contract with America, the Republican platform for the congressional elections of 1994, contained a proposal to limit welfare—not by requiring jobs after a certain time period, but by cutting off benefits completely after five years. The Contract with America plan also would have instituted a "family cap," requiring states to cut off benefits to any family that had more children while on welfare. The Republican proposal also gave states more of the flexibility they wanted, by sending them predetermined lump sum payments for welfare that states could use as they saw fit, with some restrictions. These payments, called block grants, eliminated the entitlement status of welfare. Under the AFDC program, any needy family who met the eligibility requirements would qualify for assistance, regardless of the cost. As an open-ended entitlement program, AFDC costs could vary, depending on the numbers of people who both met the requirements and applied for benefits. A block grant, on the other hand, would not only cap spending at a specified amount, but would also allow states to turn away individuals who might meet eligibility requirements—such persons would no longer be "entitled" to receive welfare.

That an end to the entitlement status was even being discussed was a sign of the shift to the right on the welfare debate. Previously, policymakers had viewed the right to assistance as sacrosanct. Now Republicans were saying that such a right encouraged dependence on welfare and discouraged individual initiative. Clinton's proposal, although conservative for a Democrat, still maintained welfare as an entitlement. One further difference between the Clinton proposal and the Republican proposal was in terms of costs. Clinton, in keeping with conclusions drawn by most policy analysts about welfare, proposed spending more money on welfare. The money would go to services intended to help welfare clients find and keep jobs: child care, training and education programs, and so forth. Although liberals are more likely to want to spend money on welfare, there was support from some conservative quarters on this issue. Republican Governor Tommy Thompson of Wisconsin, well-known for the conservative welfare reforms in his state, said that in order for welfare reform to save money in the long run, money must be spent in the short run. That is, by spending money on helping individuals find and keep jobs, those individuals would be more likely to get off of welfare and stay off, thus saving money over the long haul.

The Contract with America proposal, on the other hand, tied welfare reform to deficit reduction. Republicans reasoned that if the government spent less money on welfare benefits, recipients would be forced to look for jobs, thus saving money in both the long and short term. The Republican plan attempted to deter individuals from applying for welfare at all, in order to eliminate dependence on the system.

One other proposal floating in the policy stream didn't enter it until relatively late in the game. The National Governors' Association (NGA), an interest group made up of the 50 state governors, developed its own welfare reform proposal in February of 1996. Based in large part on the Republican bill considered in Congress in 1995 and 1996, the NGA attempted to moderate the legislation by requiring more federal spending on welfare than the Republicans had proposed and by limiting some of the more stringent requirements—for example, by making the family cap (cutting off spending if a woman had additional children while on welfare) optional for the states. The NGA proposal eventually became the basis for compromise legislation in Congress. It was more moderate than many of the House Republicans would have liked, but it was still closer to Contract with America recommendations than to the Clinton legislation. The governors, who had been asking for increased flexibility on welfare for years, liked the concept of the block grant, since it allowed states (rather than the federal government) to determine eligibility requirements for welfare. However, the governors felt that their flexibility was limited in the Republican bill because it would have required states to enforce the family cap and because it had strict work requirements. The governors' proposal gave states more room to maneuver, as well as more money to spend on welfare. The NGA proposal became particularly important in the process because it was seen as a compromise, agreed to by both Republican and Democratic governors. If governors from both parties could agree to welfare legislation, then Congress and the president could be expected to come to some agreement as well.

The Political Stream

Although a problem was evident with welfare and there were some solutions available to solve the problem, there was no guarantee that welfare reform would pass in the 104th Congress. In the first place, the solutions proposed by the president and the congressional Republicans were radically different, and it was not at all clear that any kind of middle ground could be struck. The political stream, that is, the political environment in which policies are made, is always of utmost importance in passage of legislation. If the time isn't right politically, legislation may be stalled for months or years, or may even be dropped altogether. In early 1996, it looked like welfare reform would not be enacted.

There was one major reason why the political stream opened up a policy window in the summer of 1996: the fact that 1996 was an election year. The

Republican majority that had swept into Congress under the Contract with America was finding that it had few legislative achievements that its members could campaign on in the fall elections. And President Clinton, who had been put in the awkward position of having to declare his relevance in the face of an activist Congress, could also use passage of welfare reform as a campaign issue, since he too was up for reelection. Passage of welfare reform was even more important to the president, given the dismal failure of his health care proposal. And the specter of President Bush's retreat on his "no new taxes" campaign was hanging over President Clinton's head. He did not want his campaign pledge to "end welfare as we know it" to be used against him by Republicans in the same way that Democrats had used Bush's pledge against him.

Congressional Republicans were well aware of President Clinton's pledge and of how politically valuable a third presidential veto would be for them. As the elections grew near, Republicans realized that by sending the president the welfare bill yet again, they would be forcing him into a difficult position. If he signed a Republican welfare reform bill, he would anger his liberal constituency but fulfill his campaign promise. If he vetoed the bill, he would maintain his Democratic base but he would also have to defend his decision to renege on his campaign promise. And both Democrats and Republicans knew that a broken campaign pledge would make for very effective campaign commercials, both for presidential candidate Bob Dole and for Republican members of Congress running for reelection. President Clinton could be particularly damaged by such commercials, since the public already had a tendency to perceive him as untrustworthy and vacillating. Republicans had to consider one other risk to themselves: If they sent the president a bill and he chose to sign it, he could use welfare reform as one of his legislative accomplishments, taking some of the thunder out of their campaigns.

Of course, the elections played a large part in the calculations of congressional Democrats as well. Individual Democrats, stung by the Republican victory in 1994, were afraid to vote against a popular Contract with America plank, only to have that vote thrown back in their faces in the fall election. As a whole, the Democratic congressional leadership still harbored hopes of taking back the majority in one or both houses of Congress, and they did not want welfare reform to keep them from their goal. Individual Democrats, who were generally opposed to the conservative welfare reform bill, were particularly fearful of voting against a bill that the president might eventually sign, which would obviously be used against them in their reelection campaigns. If, however, they knew that the president would veto the bill, Democrats in Congress would have more incentive to vote against it, knowing that they would have some political protection in their campaigns.

And so the political stage was set by the summer of 1996. Congressional Republicans had to decide whether giving the president the opportunity to sign a welfare reform bill was worth the legislative accomplishment. If so, the Republicans needed to come up with a bill that would offer enough cover for the president to sign, the president had to indicate to Democrats that he would sign it, and welfare as we know it could finally come to an end. The dance of legislation began in earnest.

Welfare Policy Formulation

Background

Before recounting the events of 1996 that led to final passage of welfare reform, let us briefly review where welfare stood as of May 1996. President Clinton had submitted his version of welfare reform in 1994; that bill died in the 103rd Congress. In early 1995, after the new Republican majority Congress had been sworn in, the Contract with America legislation was submitted and considered in Congress. The first version of welfare reform went through the House quickly. It passed on March 24, 1995, on a party-line vote and was sent to the Senate for consideration. The Senate, which tends to be a more moderate institution, was slower to take action. By August 1995, Majority Leader Bob Dole, anxious to produce welfare reform in the Senate, announced that he would postpone the traditional August Senate recess to work on welfare reform. Within a couple of days, however, the Senator abruptly pulled the legislation, claiming that the Democrats were putting up roadblocks to passage. "If we stayed here all night every night this week, we wouldn't finish," Dole said. "Democrats have decided it's not going to happen this week."[4] In reality, it appeared that Senate Republicans were having a difficult time coming to agreement.[5] Conservative senators wanted to pass legislation similar to the House version, which created a block grant, established a lifetime limit of five years on welfare, made deep cuts in spending on food stamps, and produced other cost savings by restricting benefits to legal immigrants. The legislation also contained the family cap requirements and denied benefits to teenage mothers. More moderate Republican senators wanted to make these provisions a state option and to spend more money on child care.[6] The moderate Republicans, aligning with moderate Democrats, were willing to compromise on the legislation in order to get a bill that the president could sign.

When the Senate finally returned to consideration of the welfare bill after Labor Day, the coalition of moderate Republican and Democratic senators won.

The bill the Senate passed on September 19, 1995, was a modified version of the House bill. It included more spending on child care and increased the amount of money that states would be required to spend on welfare. The family cap requirement was eliminated. The legislation, which was passed with Democratic support (87–12), drew praise from the president, who indicated that he could sign it. "If welfare reform remains a bipartisan effort to promote work, protect children, and collect child support from people who ought to pay it," Clinton said, "we will have welfare reform this year, and it will be a very great thing."[7] But the fight was not finished yet. Liberal Democrats were not happy with the Senate or House legislation, both of which ended the entitlement to welfare. Senator Kennedy (D–MA) spoke for the liberal Democrats when he said, "After more than 60 years of maintaining a good-faith national commitment to protect all needy children, the Senate is on the brink of committing legislative child abuse."[8] In addition, conservative Republicans were displeased with the Senate version, which they felt was too watered down and had given too many concessions to moderates.

The next venue for these disagreements to play out in was the House-Senate conference committee. When the House and Senate each pass different versions of the same bill, the legislation is sent to a conference committee, which works out the differences, coming up with a compromise bill that is then sent back to each chamber to be voted on again. In this case, the conservatives from the House wrested control of the conference committee. Many of the areas of disagreement were resolved by moving closer to the more conservative House version. Democrats, feeling that they were ignored in the process, refused to support conference committee legislation.[9] Further complicating matters, welfare reform legislation was attached to budget reconciliation legislation, which contained additional deficit reduction provisions that Clinton opposed. Clinton vetoed the budget reconciliation measure on December 6, 1995, effectively vetoing welfare reform as well.

Republicans then moved to force the president's hand. Reasoning that his veto of welfare reform could be hidden by the larger debate over deficit reduction, Republicans separated welfare reform from budget reconciliation and sent it to the president as a stand-alone bill. President Clinton was forced to veto welfare reform specifically, on January 6, 1996, exactly a month after he had indicated that he could sign the Senate legislation. Clinton defended his veto by saying that the measure was

> burdened with deep budget cuts and structural changes that fall short of real reform. I urge the Congress to work with me in good faith to produce a bipartisan welfare reform agreement that is tough on work and responsibility but not tough on children and on parents who are responsible and who want to work.[10]

The Clinton veto came while Congress was out of session and was announced at 8:00 P.M. on a snowy Washington evening. Republican leader Bob Dole called it a "stealth veto" since it was made at a time when the members of Congress and the public were unlikely to be paying close attention.[11] Nonetheless, Republicans in Congress were quick to point out that Clinton's veto meant, at least for the time being, a renouncement of his campaign promise to end the system.

The Governors Weigh In

Midway through the 104th Congress, then, Republicans had managed to pass Contract with America welfare reform, and President Clinton managed to veto it not once, but twice. It looked like ending welfare as we know it was not going to happen.

In February of 1996, however, the tide had begun to turn. The National Governors' Association's plan, as described previously, made the family cap a state option, spent more money on child care, and made work rules less restrictive. It would save about $44 billion in welfare spending over seven years, compared to the more than $64 billion the House plan would save. The plan was unanimously approved by the governors on February 6. Once the governors came to an agreement, the mood changed on the Hill. "We may have finally found a way to do business," Clay Shaw, Ways and Means Committee chairman, announced when he heard about the plan.[12]

Since the governors' proposal was not that different from the Senate bill, it seems curious that it would be cause for elation. After all, the conference committee had had the option to make some of the very changes the governors suggested but had instead chosen to go with the House bill. But the NGA is taken very seriously in Washington for at least two reasons. First, the governors, as chief executives in the states, are the ones who end up with authority for any block grant program. Since they would be the people running the block grant, Congress listened carefully to their proposals. Second, the National Governors' Association is made up of both Democrats and Republicans, and if the governors can come to an agreement, then it is perceived as a bipartisan effort. The NGA proposal was bipartisan, had an aura of expertise, and was in some ways a breath of fresh air for the bickering members of Congress. Legislators in both the House and the Senate were eager to get to work on the NGA bill, and hearings were scheduled almost immediately to discuss the proposal.

Thus, the legislative process for welfare reform, which had already come to completion once before, was started anew in the 104th Congress. Now let us turn to the path that finally led to passage of welfare reform.

Election-Year Politics

By spring of 1996, the issue of welfare reform was again becoming a focal point in Congress. The NGA proposal had become the basis for a compromise bill put together by moderate Republicans and conservative Democrats in the House. With elections looming on the horizon, members of both parties were anxious to forge a compromise that could be signed by the president and then used in campaigns as a legislative accomplishment. As Representative John Tanner, a Democrat from Tennessee, explained, "People want to go home with something to run on. You're not going to have a Democrat or Republican plan exclusive of the other party that's going to make it through this place."[13] No one was more aware of the potential of welfare reform as a campaign issue than Senator Bob Dole. By April, Dole was assured of the Republican nomination for the presidency, and he knew that his campaign could use passage of welfare reform legislation as a major legislative accomplishment. By shepherding welfare reform through the Senate, Dole's legislative and leadership skills could be highlighted. But this also put Dole in an awkward position: Passage of welfare reform would mean the fulfillment of President Clinton's by-now-famous campaign promise. If Dole could campaign on the issue of welfare reform, so too could President Clinton. On the other hand, if welfare reform remained stalled in Congress, Dole, as well as Republicans in Congress, could run against Clinton and the Democrats by making hay of the president's two previous vetoes of welfare reform.

Senator Dole was left with three choices: He could make sure that welfare reform did not get out of Congress, forcing the president to go on the defensive to explain his vetoes; he could send the president legislation that he could sign, giving both Clinton and Dole the opportunity to use welfare reform as an accomplishment to run on; or he could send the president a bill that he would likely veto, giving the Republicans an issue to attack the president on.[14] The risk of the latter strategy was that it could make both Democrats and Republicans look bad and alienate voters already angry that the two parties could not seem to compromise on a variety of issues, causing the gridlock that had temporarily shut down the government during the budget process. For the time being, Dole stuck with the first strategy of doing nothing on welfare reform.

Clouding the issue for Dole was the looming decision about how he should handle his presidential campaign. Remaining in the Senate meant he could make the most of his legislative accomplishments, including Senate passage of welfare reform legislation. On the other hand, his duties as Senate majority leader limited the time he had available for campaigning. He also sensed the anti-Washington mood of the public and felt that by resigning from the Senate, he could demonstrate his commitment to the people. In the spring of 1996, the common wisdom was that Dole would step down as majority leader in order to run his campaign. Dole actually had a more dramatic move in mind. On April 15, he announced that he would resign his Senate seat by June 11 in order to make running for president a full-time job. It was a surprise announcement. In fact, only hours before, Speaker of the House Newt Gingrich responded to a reporter's question by unequivocally stating that Dole was staying in the Senate. An embarrassed Dole had to call Gingrich to tell him the reporter had actually gotten it right.[15] When welfare reform finally moved in the 104rd Congress, Dole would not be part of the action.

President Clinton made a move to claim welfare as his issue. In his May 18 weekly radio address, the president lavished praise on a conservative welfare plan proposed by Governor Tommy Thompson of Wisconsin. Republicans quickly protested that the president's remarks were entirely politically motivated. First, the Wisconsin plan was not that different from the Republican legislation the president had vetoed a few months earlier. In addition, Clinton's speech was timed perfectly to upstage Senator Dole, who presidential advisors knew would be going to Fond du Lac, Wisconsin, three days later to make a key campaign speech on the subject of welfare. Republicans were quick to point out that the Wisconsin plan was similar to Republican congressional legislation. House Speaker Newt Gingrich, along with four other House Republicans, sent a letter to the president saying, "There is ample ground to be confused about where you stand on welfare reform," particularly since the president's administration had not yet approved the waivers necessary for the Wisconsin plan to go into effect. For his part, the president maintained the offensive. Campaigning in Milwaukee, Wisconsin, a few days after Senator Dole's speech, the president challenged the senator to send him welfare reform legislation. This time, the president said, "I will sign it, and we will put this behind us."[16]

Stalemate

In between Dole's speech in Fond du Lac and Clinton's in Milwaukee, Republicans in Congress unveiled their latest welfare overhaul on May 22. Based on the NGA proposal, the new legislation required welfare recipients to work after two years and instituted a lifetime limit of five years for benefits. It allowed the family cap at state option and provided for additional child care and "rainy day" funding (to help states out in the event of an economic downturn), as the governors wished. However, the legislation included stricter work requirements than the NGA proposal had suggested. Although at first glance the proposal seemed to provide a strong basis for compromise, the Republican bill actually showed an unwillingness to work with the president and congressional Democrats. Republicans tied welfare reform to Medicaid reform, thereby almost guaranteeing a presidential veto.

Medicaid is the health care program for the poor and disabled, which is closely tied to welfare. Although by May 1996, most Democrats had demonstrated their willingness to end the entitlement status of welfare, they were almost universally opposed to eliminating the entitlement to Medicaid. And President Clinton had specifically said he would oppose a Medicaid block grant, which the Republicans were now including in their welfare reform package. For their part, governors, particularly Republican governors, were anxious to receive Medicaid as a block grant. As an entitlement, Medicaid sent federal funds to the states for medical assistance to the poor, but it also required the states to "match" federal money by spending a certain percentage of state money as well. Under a block grant, states would not receive as much federal money, but they also wouldn't be required to spend as much money either. Thus states were strongly in favor of Medicaid reform as a cost-cutting measure for themselves. And Republicans in Congress strongly supported increasing state flexibility on Medicaid as well as on welfare.

But Democrats were just as strongly in favor of maintaining the entitlement to Medicaid. Although most Democrats were willing to accept that welfare recipients should no longer expect a lifetime guarantee of benefits, they were not willing to eliminate the limited guarantees of health care coverage for the poor. Liberals felt that Medicaid revisions would end what minimal obligations the federal government was maintaining to protect its poorest citizens. In fact Clinton, who had proposed universal health coverage, would have liked to extend Medicaid coverage for welfare recipients who got jobs, thus easing their transition to work. By tying welfare reform, for which there was now the possibility of compromise acceptable to both parties, to Medicaid reform, about which the two parties were clearly at odds, the Republicans appeared to be taunting the president and liberal Democrats. And nowhere was the political situation more clear than in the press conference at which the bill was unveiled: Only Republicans were present. On the sidelines, Democrats complained that they had been left out of the process in developing the legislation. The bipartisan approach begun by the governors had evaporated in the election year atmosphere. Republicans had decided not to give the president a bill he could sign, instead deciding to attack him on the campaign trail for neglecting to keep his promise on welfare. Governor Howard Dean of Vermont, a

Democrat, summed up the Democrats' attitude toward the new legislation. "It's basically bait and switch," he said. "It's clearly just a strategy to force President Clinton to veto another bill so they can go on the airwaves with it."[17]

The Clinton administration still maintained its willingness to compromise. Testifying for the Department of Health and Human Services, Assistant Secretary Mary Jo Bane told members of Congress, "The president has made it quite clear that if Congress sends him a clean welfare bill that requires work, that promotes responsibility, and that protects children, he will sign it."[18] By a "clean" bill, Bane obviously meant one that did not come with Medicaid provisions attached. In the meantime, House and Senate committees prepared to begin markup of the welfare-Medicaid legislation in June.

Legitimation of Welfare Policy

Congress Takes the Lead

Congressional Republicans also figured out a way to get back at Clinton for taking control of the welfare issue in Wisconsin. Although Clinton had praised the state's welfare reform bill, his administration had not yet approved the necessary waivers. In order to steal the issue back, the House decided to take the unusual move of voting to give Wisconsin the waivers. Normally, the executive agencies grant requests for such waivers. In its legislative role, Congress passes the broad outlines of a policy, and then the executive function of filling in the parameters through rules and regulations is done by the executive branch. Waiving the rules is generally considered an executive function. For the scores of waivers that had been approved since the Reagan administration, Congress had never felt the need to pass a law. In this case, it was politics that motivated House Republican leaders. By taking such a vote, they could point out the fact that Clinton had not acted and, in turn, make it clear that Congress was the center of activity on welfare reform. Although the waiver bill passed on June 6 (289–136, with 60 Democrats and all Republicans supporting it), the legislation had very little chance of passage in the Senate.

House Consideration

In the meantime, the welfare reform bill was winding its way through the committee process in the House. The committee system organizes both houses of Congress. The House and Senate both have divided their work into substantive policy areas (such as education, transportation, and commerce) that provide

TABLE 3.3   Welfare Committees and Their Jurisdiction

Committees	Jurisdiction
House Committees	
Agriculture	Food stamps
Commerce	Revisions to Medicaid
Economic and Educational Opportunities	Work, child care, child nutrition
Ways and Means	AFDC, SSI, Medicaid eligibility
Budget	Puts pieces of bill together as part of budget reconciliation process
Rules	Schedules bill for floor debate
Senate Committees	
Agriculture, Nutrition, and Forestry	Food stamps
Finance	AFDC, Medicaid, Earned Income Tax Credit
Budget	Puts pieces of bill together as part of budget reconciliation process

the jurisdiction for committees. Bills are sent to the committees—and then referred to subcommittees—with appropriate jurisdiction in each house. This process is called *referral*. In the House, three committees had jurisdiction over welfare: the Committee on Agriculture, which dealt with the food stamps portion of the bill; the Committee on Economic and Educational Opportunities, which had jurisdiction over requirements, child care, and child nutrition provisions; and the Committee on Ways and Means, which had jurisdiction over almost everything else. In addition, the Commerce Committee had jurisdiction over the Medicaid provisions (see Table 3.3).

In early June, House committees marked up welfare legislation. *Markup* is the process in which committees consider legislation, going over it line by line, and offering committee members the opportunity to propose *amendments*, or changes in the language of the bill. Welfare reform first went to the Human Resources Subcommittee of the Ways and Means Committee for markup. Subcommittee Democrats proposed several amendments. One would have instituted vouchers for diapers, school supplies, and other necessities for children whose parents were eliminated from welfare due to the new time limits. Democrats insisted that providing vouchers—which could be redeemed only for appropriate purchases—were necessary to help children, while still denying their parents extra cash. Another Democratic amendment would have restored some assistance to legal immigrants: Under the Republican plan, legal aliens residing in the United States for less than ten years would be ineligible. The Democratic alternative would make exceptions for those already eligible for assistance at the time of the bill's passage. Both amendments failed. On June 5, the subcommittee *reported out* the legislation. That is, the subcommittee approved the bill and sent it to the next stage of the process, in this case, to full committee consideration.

The "full committee" was the Committee on Ways and Means, which marked up the bill on June 12. The first action in the committee was a vote on a Democratic substitute, approved by President Clinton and offered as a replacement amendment—replacing the entire bill. The amendment failed. The Republican bill ultimately passed in the committee by a vote of 23 to 14, with only one Democrat (Gerald Kleczka of Wisconsin) voting in favor. The Ways and Means Committee then reported out the bill, signifying that it was ready for floor consideration. However, since the bill was simultaneously being considered by other committees (this is called *multiple referral* because the bill is referred to more than one committee at a time), floor action had to wait until the remaining committees reported out their versions. Within a couple of days, the Agriculture Committee and Economic and Educational Opportunities Committee had reported out their versions of the welfare provisions, and the Commerce Committee had reported out the Medicaid portion of the bill.

As of June 13, three committees had reported slightly different versions of the welfare reform provisions, and a fourth had reported the Medicaid provisions. The legislation still wasn't ready for floor consideration, however. Since welfare reform was part of a larger deficit reduction plan (changes in the law would create substantial cost savings that would help lower the deficit), the Budget Committee had to review the bill. The budget committee's role was not to change the substance of the bill; rather, it had to certify that the four committees had met its instructions for deficit reduction. On June 19, the Budget Committee approved the joint welfare-Medicaid legislation, signifying it was ready for floor consideration.

However, there was one more hurdle the bill had to get over. Just about every piece of major legislation must be considered by the Rules Committee before it is sent to the House floor. Like the Budget Committee, the Rules Committee does not usually review the substance of a bill. Rather, it debates the *rule* for the bill, which schedules the bill for floor debate and sets the terms of the debate. In mid-June, the bill stopped there. Before floor debate could be scheduled in the House, the leadership wanted to see what would happen in the Senate.

Senate Consideration

Even as committee action was dying down in the House, it was heating up in the Senate. On the same day that the House Budget Committee approved the welfare reform legislation, the Senate Agriculture Committee voted on the food stamp portion of the bill. Like the House, the Senate refers bills to committee based on jurisdiction. In the Senate, only two committees had jurisdiction over welfare reform: the Agriculture Committee (which dealt with food stamps) and the Senate Finance Committee (which dealt with everything else, including Medicaid). On June 26, the Senate Finance Committee marked up the legislation. First, the committee voted to defeat a voucher proposal, similar to the one defeated in the House. Senator Baucus (D–MT) then proposed an amendment to strip the Medicaid provisions from the bill. The amendment failed, opposed by all Republicans and six of the committee's nine Democrats. The vote on this amendment was pure political strategy. Republicans wanted to keep Medicaid and welfare reform joined to ensure a presidential veto that they could campaign on; Democrats wanted a presidential veto because they felt that (particularly with the defeat of the voucher proposal) the bill was too stringent, and they were afraid of presidential approval of a bill they did not like. Eventually, the Senate Finance Committee added amendments moderating the changes to Medicaid, while still ending its entitlement status.

Within days, the Medicaid portion of the bill was in trouble. First, Republican governors placed a phone call on July 9 to congressional leaders to protest the Medicaid amendments just passed.[19] Whereas liberal Democrats were unhappy because the amendments ended the federal government's obligation to provide Medicaid, Republican governors felt the amendments did not provide states enough flexibility. Essentially, the Republican leadership was being pummeled from both sides: Liberals said the provisions went too far, while conservatives said they didn't go far enough. In addition, Republicans in Congress were rethinking the political implications of their strategy to tie Medicaid to welfare reform. More and more Republican members, especially the freshmen (elected under the Contract with America and facing their first reelection campaigns), were coming to the conclusion that they should present President Clinton with a bill he could sign. Finally Senator Dole, confined to the sidelines of the debate since he had resigned a month earlier, sent a letter to the Republican leadership, urging them to pass welfare reform legislation.[20] The policy window for passing welfare reform was about to open up.

Congress Passes a Bill

On July 11, 1996, Republican congressional leaders announced that they would split welfare reform legislation from Medicaid. Bill Archer, chairman of the House Ways and Means Committee, taunted Clinton: "Mr. President, we're calling your bluff," he said. "It's time to either put up or stop the rhetoric."[21] For his part, the president was sending mixed signals. On July 16, in a statement broadcast by satellite to an NGA meeting in Puerto Rico, President Clinton announced, "I think we have now reached a real turning point, a breakthrough for welfare reform."[22] Days later, the president sent a letter to Congress criticizing the welfare bill and supporting a more moderate Democratic alternative. Clinton's letter faulted the Republican bill for not providing enough health coverage to people kicked off of welfare, for making too many cuts in spending on food stamps, and for including too many restrictions on legal immigrants receiving benefits.[23] Speaker of the House Newt Gingrich responded to the president with his own letter, saying in part, "Welfare reform must include a general ban on benefits for noncitizens."[24] For his part, the Senate minority leader, Democrat Tom Daschle, told reporters, "I think the president made it abundantly clear to Dick [Gephardt, House minority leader] and to me . . . that he will veto a bad bill. There is a notion out there that somehow, the president is prepared to sign virtually anything."[25]

Meanwhile, the House had been spurred to action on the bill. Up until this time welfare reform had been stalled in the House. The bill needed to be sent to the Rules Committee to schedule floor consideration, but House leaders put it on hold while they waited for signals from the president and the Senate. Now that the bill had passed through the committees in the Senate, and the House and Senate leadership had negotiated a maneuver to encourage a presidential signature (by detaching the Medicaid provisions), and the president had indicated that he might actually sign a bill, the House was finally ready to move welfare reform to the floor. The Rules Committee held its hearing on July 17, after the House leadership had decided on a "modified closed rule" for floor consideration of the bill. A *closed rule* means that no amendments from the floor are allowed; an *open rule* means that amendments are unlimited; and a *modified closed rule* allows a restricted number of amendments. Once the form of the rule has been decided, the House votes on it as a resolution on the floor. If the rule passes, floor consideration begins. If it fails, then the bill cannot be considered, and it has been effectively killed—before it has even been debated!

The rule for welfare reform legislation passed on July 18, and floor consideration began immediately. The House resolved into the *Committee of the Whole,* a procedural device under which legislation is considered. When the House is acting as the Committee of the Whole, its quorum is not a simple majority (218 members) but 100 members, making debate less cumbersome. The bill was restricted to two hours of debate, with Republicans and Democrats allowed an hour each. Debate was controlled by the chair and ranking minority member of the House Budget Committee. Before the final vote, the Democratic alternative that President Clinton favored was proposed as a "replacement amendment" (replacing the entire bill with a new version), but it was voted down, 258–168. The day before consideration, the Clinton administration had asked Democrats in the House to vote against the Republican bill, to give the White House more leverage in later negotiations. By the end of the day, the bill had passed, 256–170, with all but 30 Democrats following the president's instructions.

The White House picked up the issue immediately, continuing to send mixed signals. Presidential spokesman Mike McCurry said that the bill was better than the legislation that Clinton had vetoed in December and January, implying that the president could sign the new bill.[26] The following Sunday, Vice President Gore said on the television news show "Face the Nation" that although the president had no objections to ending the entitlement status of welfare, he would prefer a bill that included vouchers for children whose parents are removed from the rolls because of time limits.[27]

In the meantime, the Senate had begun its deliberations on July 18. Whereas bills in the House must go through the Rules Committee before floor consideration can begin, there is no such committee in the Senate. Instead, the Senate brings bills to the floor under a *unanimous consent agreement,* negotiated between minority and majority leaders. The Senate had received the House bill, passed the unanimous consent agreement, and begun floor consideration by first passing an amendment to replace all language in the House bill with the Senate language that had already been winding its way through committees. Its next move was to approve, by voice vote, an amendment by Majority Leader Trent Lott (who had replaced Dole the month before) to detach the Medicaid provisions from the bill. Senator Dole, now facing the consequences of his decision to leave the Senate, attempted to keep his hand in the process. At a summit in the Great Lakes region, he made a public statement to three Midwestern Republican governors: "I have a feeling that [President Clinton] will sign anything with welfare reform on it; I may be wrong, but that's why we need to make certain that whatever goes to him is a good solid bill. We have to make certain he gets another crack at it. We have to give him one more strike."[28] The next day, July 23, the Senate approved the welfare bill by a 74–24 vote, with 23 Democrats in favor and 23 against. Four amendments that were important to President Clinton were voted on; only two passed. The Senate agreed to extend Medicaid to individuals who lose benefits because of new eligibility restrictions and to retain the entitlement status of the food stamp program. The Senate failed to approve an amendment allowing vouchers for children whose families lose benefits and an amendment allowing aid to legal immigrants.[29]

Clinton now sounded like he might not sign the bill. Responding to the Senate action, he again gave mixed signals, saying, "You can put wings on a pig, but you don't make it an eagle. We want real welfare reform." On the other hand, he said, "Today the Senate took some major steps to improve the bill going through Congress. If we can keep this progress up, if we can make it bipartisan, then we can have a real welfare reform bill that honors work and protects children."[30] But Clinton still held out hope that he could get changes to the bill. In order for legislation to pass Congress and be sent to the president, it must be reported out of both houses in identical form. Since the House and Senate had passed different versions of the same bill, it was sent to a *conference committee*, made up of members of both chambers. The purpose of the conference committee is to work out differences between two versions of the same bill. Normally, the conference committee limits itself to areas of disagreement in the two bills. The Clinton administration hoped that the committee might make an exception this time since the president wanted two things that weren't included in either bill: the voucher program for children and reinstatement of benefits to legal immigrants.

Republicans in Congress decided to play hardball with the president. In a memo to one of his aides, Gingrich said, "I believe the White House will sign just about anything we send them, so we should make them eat as much as we can."[31] The president expressed his desire to sign a bill in his weekly radio address but would not specify what would make him veto a bill. He, too, was playing politics. He was afraid that if he was specific, Republicans would use his words against him, by including provisions that would force a veto. The president appeared to be prepared to sign a bill that was like the Senate version, veto one like the House version. All along, conference committee action was running relatively smoothly. Formal negotiations began on July 25, and Democrats felt more included in the process than they had in the previous round in the fall of 1995. "They're treating us a whole lot better than they've treated us before," Charlie Stenholm (D–TX) said of the Republicans at the conference.[32]

House and Senate conferees reached agreement on July 29, 1996. The bill they reported was closer to the Senate bill. The president now had to make a decision. Would he sign welfare reform or veto it? Liberal interest groups tried to encourage a veto. At a joint news conference, the National Urban League, the Children's Defense Fund, the National Conference of Bishops, and the Union of American Hebrew Congregations denounced the bill and urged a presidential veto. Congressional Democrats awaited the president's decision. The conference bill would be sent back to both the House and Senate for a floor vote, and Democrats needed to know what the president was going to do. Many Democrats, especially the more liberal ones, wouldn't mind voting against the bill. But if they did so and the president signed it, they would likely be branded extremists by Republican opponents in their reelection campaigns. Congress awaited the president's decision with bated breath.

The next morning, August 1, President Clinton called his advisors to the Cabinet Room. In a somewhat subdued two-and-a-half-hour meeting, the president asked opponents and proponents of the bill within his administration to make their final case. On the "veto" side were all the members of the president's cabinet, including Donna Shalala, Secretary of Health and Human Services. George Stephanopoulous, who had been with Clinton since the 1992 campaign, also opposed the bill, as did Leon Panetta, Clinton's chief of staff. They listed their objections to the bill: It was too extreme; it abdicated the federal government's sixty-year obligation to the poor; it did not have enough safety valves to help people thrown off of welfare under new restrictive regulations; it would pull the safety net out from under thousands of families that needed governmental assistance. On the other side were most of Clinton's political advisors, as well as Vice President Al Gore. His domestic policy advisor, Bruce Reed, and political advisors Dick Morris (not present at the morning meeting) and Rahm Emmanuel had been outspoken defenders of the bill.[33] The bill was not so bad, Reed argued. It encouraged work and was consistent with the president's original intention of time-limiting welfare. Besides, if the Democrats won back control of Congress, there would be ample opportunity to fine-tune the bill and make its provisions less draconian.

Although the discussion at the meeting revolved around the merits of the bill, everyone understood the political implications lurking beneath the surface. Bruce Reed told the president, "We made a promise to the people in 1992 to end welfare as we know it. This bill isn't perfect, but it keeps that promise. We would have a hard time explaining to the American people why we didn't do it."[34] If the President vetoed the bill, it would be used against him in the elections and would be one more example of his waffling. Republicans would have a heyday with Clinton's inability to fulfill a prominent campaign promise and his general failure at shepherding legislation through Congress. The general public was pretty much disgusted with the current welfare system, and a veto of its overhaul would be difficult to explain. It's no surprise that the proponents of the bill were the president's political advisors. They understood how welfare might undermine his chances at reelection and were not willing to take the risk. The president's policy advisors, on the other hand, were ideologically opposed to the bill. Many of them had spent their professional lives creating and expanding policies to help the country's least well-off citizens. They knew that even though the president had promised to end welfare as we know it, he had also promised to take care of America's poor children. They were most concerned with his breaking the latter promise. Being more ideological than political, they felt that it was incumbent upon the president to stand up for the poor by vetoing the bill. Deep down, they felt that the president could articulate his objections to the Republican welfare reform and that a veto really wouldn't cost him the election.

Clinton listened as the two camps presented their sides. Finally, at around 12:30 P.M., he got up to leave the room. "Okay, listen," he said, "I've worked on this for 16 years, I'm going to go into my office and make up my mind."[35] He disappeared into the oval office, taking Panetta and Gore with him. Fifteen minutes later, Panetta emerged and, with a grim look on his face, went to the president's speechwriters and told them to finish the "yes" speech.[36]

Congressional leaders were waiting impatiently. At 12:50 P.M., David Bonior, not knowing what was going on in the White House, told reporters, "We are all waiting for the president's decision before we can go into action."[37] The vote would not be held until Clinton announced whether he would sign or veto. At 2:26 P.M., the president finally made his announcement. In a televised speech, the president explained his decision: Although he did not like all aspects of the bill, it was the best that could be expected out of Congress "for a long, long time." He would sign the bill and work on fine-tuning it after the election. At 5:00 P.M., voting in the House began. The conference bill passed, 300–100. Democrats were split down the middle: Half voted in favor, the other half against. The next day, the Senate held its final debates on the bill. The vote was 78–21, with 25 Democrats in favor and 21 opposed. Of the Democratic senators up for reelection, only one voted against the bill (see Tables 3.4 and 3.5).

Three weeks later, President Clinton signed the welfare bill in a Rose Garden ceremony, surrounded by more congressional Republicans than Democrats. Many Democratic leaders begged off attending the festivities since most didn't really view the occasion as cause for celebration. In addition, advocates for women and children staged protests outside the White House. Clinton remained upbeat. "Today we are taking a historic chance to make welfare what it was meant to be," he said, "a second chance, not a way of life." Bob Dole, attempting to get involved in the process despite his resignation from the Senate, responded to Clinton's announcement in televised comments. Dole and his advisors took a cynical view of the president's change of heart on welfare reform. "By selling out his own party, Bill Clinton has proven he is ideologically adrift," a Dole staffer said.[38] And that sums up the dilemma for Democrats in

TABLE 3.4   How the Welfare Bill Became Law—the Textbook Version

HOUSE		SENATE
Bill introduced, referred to committees		
Human Resources Subcommittee approves bill	June 5, 1996	
Agriculture Committee considers bill	June 11, 1996	
Ways and Means Committee approves bill	June 12, 1996	
Economic and Educational Opportunities Committee approves bill		
Agriculture Committee approves bill	June 13, 1996	
Commerce Committee approves bill		
Budget Committee certifies that bill fulfills deficit-reduction requirements	June 19, 1996	Agriculture Committee approves bill
	June 26, 1996	Finance Committee approves bill
Bill placed on House Union calendar	June 27, 1996	Budget Committee certifies that bill fulfills deficit-reduction requirements
Rules Committee issues rule	July 17, 1996	
House floor debate and passage	July 18, 1996	Unanimous consent agreement approved
	July 23, 1996	Senate floor debate and final passage
Conference Committee Action July 25–30, 1996		
House agrees to conference report	July 31, 1996	
	August 1, 1996	Senate agrees to conference report
Bill presented to president August 19, 1996		
President signs the bill August 22, 1996		

TABLE 3.5   How the Welfare Bill Became Law—The Inside Story

November 1992	Bill Clinton is elected president after promising to "end welfare as we know it."
1994	President Clinton's first major legislative initiative, health care reform, dies in Congress.
Fall 1994	Clinton sends Congress his second major legislative initiative, welfare reform, which ultimately dies in Congress.
November 1994	Republicans sweep Congress under the Contract with America, which promises to save money with time-limited welfare reform.
January 1995	Republicans introduce the Personal Responsibility Act in Congress.
December 1995	President Clinton vetoes the Republican welfare reform bill as part of a larger deficit reduction measure.
January 1996	Congress strips welfare reform from the deficit reduction bill and sends it to President Clinton, who is forced to veto it as a stand-alone measure; Senator Dole calls it a "stealth veto" since the president does it at night, during a snowstorm.
February 1996	The National Governors' Association proposes a compromise bill.
April 1996	Majority Leader Bob Dole announces he will resign his Senate seat in order to run for president.
	President Clinton and Senator Dole make speeches in Wisconsin celebrating the state's conservative welfare reform.
May 1996	Republicans introduce a compromise measure based on the NGA proposal; they also tie Medicaid reform to welfare reform. Democrats (including the president) are adamant about wanting to keep the two separate.
	Republicans seem to want to send the president a bill he won't sign, forcing him to renege on his 1992 campaign promise.
	In an effort to embarrass the president, House Republicans pass a bill granting waivers to Wisconsin for its welfare reform plan; such waivers are normally issued by the executive branch.
June 1996	The Senate Finance Committee approves Medicaid provisions that neither Democratic nor Republican governors like.
July 1996	Republican governors, in a phone call with congressional leaders, express their disapproval of the Medicaid provisions.
	Former Senator Dole sends a letter to Senate Republicans, urging them to pass welfare reform.

(continues)

TABLE 3.5   *(continued)*

	Senate Republican leaders remove Medicaid provisions from welfare bill; President Clinton indicates he might now sign the legislation. Republicans now seem more interested in using welfare reform for their own reelection purposes than to force the president to go back on his promise.
	Clinton sends a letter to Congress criticizing its welfare bill; House Speaker Newt Gingrich sends a letter to the president insisting that welfare reform include a ban on benefits to legal immigrants.
	The House and Senate pass welfare reform legislation; the bill goes to conference committee and is sent back to both chambers.
	Leaders in the House and Senate await the president's announcement as to whether he will sign the legislation before their final vote on the conference bill.
August 1996	President Clinton announces he will sign welfare reform. The House and Senate vote on final passage. The bill is signed on August 22, 1996.
November 1996	President Clinton is reelected; Congress maintains its Republican majority.

the 1996 welfare reform debate: They were faced with voting against (or, in the president's case, vetoing) welfare reform legislation that went against their deeply held beliefs or going along with the popular will, as expressed by the Republicans. They chose the latter.

Welfare as we knew it had ended.

4

....

Welfare Policy in American Politics: From Rhetoric to Reform

Diffused through every layer of government, partly public, partly private, partly mixed; incomplete and still not universal; defeating its own objectives, American welfare practice is incoherent and irrational. Still this crazy system resists fundamental change.

Michael B. Katz, *In the Shadow of the Poorhouse*

Our system of welfare was created during the Great Depression, expanded during the War on Poverty, limited in the 1980s, and has been substantially revised and refocused by the Personal Responsibility and Work Opportunity Reconciliation Act (PRWORA) of 1996 and the Temporary Assistance to Needy Families (TANF) block grant it creates. Welfare does not seem to have solved the problem of poverty through the course of its history, and some contend that welfare has actually reinforced the cycle of poverty. Each attempt at reforming the welfare system has spawned later attempts at reform. Each reform addresses problems within the welfare system, sometimes to the point where the initial problem—poverty—seems peripheral. Thus, the problem that policymakers are currently addressing is not so much poverty as it is welfare. And until very recently, welfare reform has involved incremental changes.

With the passage of the PRWORA, policymakers have introduced significant changes in the assumptions underlying our welfare system. First, the PRWORA readjusts the federal-state balance for welfare toward state governments. This change in balance actually has been going on since the 1980s, when President Reagan began the waiver process through which states could experiment with various types of welfare reform. From colonial times through the 1960s, the trend was in the opposite direction, with the federal government gradually assuming more responsibility for welfare, while maintaining state administration of the program. The PRWORA still gives the federal government responsibility for providing funds to the states and establishing the parameters within which states must operate their welfare programs, but, by creating the TANF block grant, it gives the states more flexibility to create their own rules. It also puts a cap on funding, which ends the entitlement status of welfare. Prior to passage of the PRWORA, states were required to provide benefits to any additional person who qualified; the federal government guaranteed funds. With a closed-ended block grant, states now may be forced to cut benefits to additional beneficiaries once federal funding runs out.

The PRWORA also stresses the role of individual responsibility in alleviating poverty. At least since the New Deal, one of the underlying assumptions about welfare has been that poverty is a structural problem that requires governmental assistance. The PRWORA assumes instead that poverty is due in large part to lack of individual initiative and that government programs have eroded such initiative. The PRWORA hopes to encourage personal responsibility by requiring work after two years and limiting lifetime benefits to five years. The emphasis under the PRWORA is more on *employment* assistance and less on *cash* assistance.

Whether or not the latest attempt at reforming the welfare system will provide a satisfactory resolution remains to be seen. In this chapter, we examine the Personal Responsibility and Work Opportunity Reconciliation Act in the context of the welfare dilemma: Should the program focus on alleviating poverty or on reducing dependency? First, the chapter considers the problem of poverty, which is what welfare programs are designed to alleviate. The chapter then moves to a discussion of how the debate shifted to the right, and why critics wanted to "end welfare as we know it." Finally the chapter examines how the PRWORA addresses problems in the welfare system.

The Problem of Poverty

Poverty has been part of American life since the earliest days of our history, and some level of governmental assistance has always gone to the poor. One of the first problems in providing this assistance is to determine who exactly is poor. We all know that "poor" means not having enough money, but how much money is enough? Since 1955, the government has had an official poverty line, a definition of income below which a family is considered poor. The poverty line is calculated by estimating how much money a family would need annually to buy food at a minimum level of nutrition and then multiplying that amount by three.[1] The poverty rate throughout the late 1950s stayed at about 22 percent of the total population (about 39.5 million poor persons). By 1992, the poverty rate was 14.5 percent, which translates into 36.8 million people in poverty. Of those, 13.6 million, or 37 percent, received AFDC benefits.[2] The poverty line in 1993 was set at $14,763 for a family of three, which is slightly less than the $16,000 that the majority of Americans believed necessary for a family of three, according to a Gallup poll taken that year.[3]

The poverty line is itself controversial. In addition to the fact that it is generally less than what most people feel is necessary to live on, the method by which it is calculated is the subject of some debate. At the time that the poverty line was first defined, most families used approximately one-third of their annual income for food purchases. Today, families do not use such a high pro-

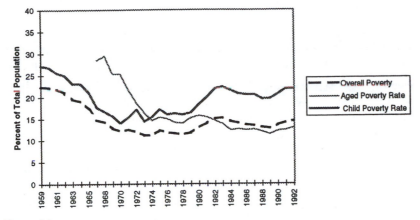

Figure 4.1
Poverty rate for individuals in selected demographic groups, 1959–1992
SOURCE: U.S. Congress, House Committee on Ways and Means, *Overview of Entitlement Programs: 1994 Greenbook,* Appendix H, p. 5.

portion of their income for food because they are spending much larger percentages on other living expenses, particularly housing and transportation. Because of the way it is calculated, the poverty line has risen at a much slower rate than average family incomes, resulting in a poverty line that is now about one-third of median family income, instead of one-half, as it was in the 1960s.[4]

Using the poverty line as a measure, the percentage of people in poverty has decreased since the early 1960s, as shown in Figure 4.1. The overall poverty rate increased slightly in the 1980s. During that period, the poverty rate for the aged was decreasing, while the poverty rate for children was increasing. As of 1992, more than a fifth of all children were in poverty, down from more than a quarter of all children in 1960. Critics from both the right and the left say that the poverty rate is an inaccurate measure of poverty. Since AFDC and other government assistance have been included in determining income, many more individuals would be classified as poor if not for government aid. If AFDC were not counted as income, 7 million more people would have been added to the poverty population in 1992, bringing the number of poor from 36.8 million to 43.8 million.[5] Liberals say that this is evidence that government aid works; conservatives say that the poverty rate demonstrates the failure of Great Society programs. In addition, liberals believe that if the poverty line were recalculated to reflect realistic needs of a family, then millions more adults and children would be classified as poor.

Another problem is often referred to as the *feminization of poverty.* More women than men fall under the poverty line, and most of the families in poverty are headed by single women. Female-headed families present difficulties for resolving the poverty problem because single mothers are responsible for both taking care of their children and earning enough money to keep their families afloat. Often, single mothers have relatively few marketable skills, especially if they were teenagers when they started their families. In addition, even if these women can find jobs, they then have to contend with child care, which is often expensive, particularly if the mother wants, as most parents do, high-quality care for her children. Often, the cost of child care alone eats up a huge portion of a working mother's paycheck. Also, when children get sick, many day care centers require them to stay at home to prevent spreading illness to the other children. Mothers then may be forced to miss work to take care of their children. And, if a single mother is in a low-skill, low-wage job, any opportunity she had for education or training programs to increase her skills would only add to her child care woes since most such programs would require her to spend more time outside of the home. Finally, many low-skill, low-wage jobs do not provide adequate health care coverage, and single mothers have found that staying on welfare not only allows them to stay home and take care of their children, but also to qualify for Medicaid, which provides health care coverage for their families.

Although putting welfare recipients to work is one way to get them out of poverty, this creates pressure on the low-wage labor market and may displace other nonwelfare workers. As former welfare recipients come into the job market, often with subsidies from the government to their employers, they may take low-wage jobs away from the working poor and keep wages low by flooding the job market.

> With the American economy thriving and unemployment low, employers frequently find themselves scrambling to find enough entry-level workers. Normally they raise wages to lure people who would not otherwise be willing to take these jobs. But with the injection of so many welfare recipients as workers, the wage pressure is dulled.[6]

Efforts to help move welfare recipients into jobs often include subsidized day care and health care for a several-month "transition period," after which the former recipients are expected to take care of these things on their own. Aside from the issue of whether or not the welfare recipients will be able to afford child care after the transition period, there is also the issue of fairness to other working poor, who do not receive such assistance (although they may qualify for the Earned Income Tax Credit [EITC], which provides for tax deductions for child care expenses).

How the Welfare Debate Moved to the Right

The welfare system established in 1935 focused on the goal of assistance. Social programs, including ADC, unemployment compensation, and social security, were designed to help the poor. Assistance was a popular goal for three reasons. First, pretty much everyone agreed during the depression that the poor were truly needy. The problem was not within the people themselves; rather, it was in the structure of the economy. A collapsed economy displaced everyone, including hard-working, responsible people. Second, poverty programs, especially the work relief programs set up by the New Deal, were viewed as temporary. Even President Roosevelt, to whom we look as the architect of the current welfare state, thought that as the economy recovered, the need for work relief would "wither away."[7] This structural interpretation of the poverty problem was appealing precisely because it implied that the problem was temporary. Thus welfare programs often had the word "relief" in them. Finally, ADC, which was intended as a permanent program for widows and their families, was initially popular since worthy widows "deserved" assistance, and women were assumed to be dependent on their husbands.

By the time the Great Society was established in the 1960s, policymakers had ceased expecting the welfare state to wither away. In fact, they wanted to expand it. The popular perception, among policymakers at least, was that poverty was a permanent structural problem—not just a result of a collapsed economy, but the result of the capitalistic system itself. It was unrealistic to expect that everyone could rise to the top, even in times of economic growth. Scholars pointed to the widespread occurrence of abject poverty, even in our advanced industrial country. If viewed as a structural problem, there are two ways to deal with poverty. One is to change the structure, in this case, the system of capitalism. Clearly, this would not be possible in the United States. The other way to deal with poverty is to provide assistance, as had been attempted in some of the New Deal programs. Accepting that poverty will always exist in a capitalistic economy, policymakers could simply provide monetary or material assistance to help the plight of the poor.

Interestingly, the Great Society, which had as its theoretical basis the structural interpretation of poverty, did not attempt to change the structure or merely provide assistance. Instead, policymakers settled on the goal of *rehabilitation.* That is, they would give those in poverty the skills they needed to become successful participants in the economy. Although this is an admirable goal, it did not square with the broader theory policymakers were propounding: that the capitalistic economy left a certain number of people behind.[8] That is, if poverty is a result of a structural problem, no amount of rehabilitation will eliminate poverty entirely. And the elimination of poverty, by creating and expanding opportunities for the poor to help themselves, was the intent of the Great Society.

During the 1960s and 1970s, the debate about welfare existed to the left of center. There was a general assumption that governmental programs were good, not only for their intended purposes, but also for the money that government spending pumped into the economy. Welfare was a "liberal" issue, and although conservatives complained about welfare spending and fraud in the program, they tended to focus their energies elsewhere. That changed in the 1980s, due to three interrelated factors. First, the Keynesian notion of "priming the pump" took a hit from "supply-side" economics, which said that a better way of infusing money into the economy was to reduce inflation and encourage savings. The best way to do this, according to supply-siders, was to cut taxes and decrease government spending. Cutting taxes for individuals at higher income levels encouraged more savings, fueling increased economic growth.[9] Second, there was a backlash against 1960s ideology. The programs set up in the 1960s were criticized for creating huge bureaucracies, for not accomplishing their stated goals, and for basically being a waste of taxpayers' money. This backlash created a public that was happy to test supply-side economics. Third, starting with Nixon in the 1970s, federal policymakers began to talk seriously about giving more authority to the states. The increasing power of the federal government, they believed, was one of the key reasons for the problems with the Great Society programs. So policymakers began to propose sending various programs back to the states, which, as the "laboratories of democracy," were the best place to run social programs anyway.

As the public became more unhappy with government, the door was opened for conservatives to enter the welfare debate. First, Reagan suggested creating an optional welfare block grant that would give states flexibility to spend federal funds—an idea that was considered so ludicrous at the time that even members of his own administration spoke out against it.[10] That very idea is one of the fundamental tenets of the Personal Responsibility and Work Opportunity Reconciliation Act, which, as we saw in Chapter 3, passed both houses of Congress with bipartisan support and was signed by a Democratic president. But the fact that Reagan made welfare a policy priority—he suggested a reform of the welfare system in his January 1986 State of the Union address—brought conservatives into the debate on welfare. Conservatives were also fueled by a book published in 1984 by Charles Murray, called *Losing Ground*, which criticized Great Society programs for creating dependency and long-term poverty.[11] The 1988 Family Support Act was the result of a new consensus on welfare—that recipients should be required to work and that they should receive increased support-ive services, such as child care and transportation, to help them do so. Liberals were happy with the supportive services, conservatives, with the work require-ments. Welfare policy had found a moderate position.

Americans have always been wary of government spending on welfare. We think the government should spend money on the truly needy but want to make sure that "undeserving" individuals don't tap into that money. "It is only a slight exaggeration to say that the core of most welfare reform in America since the early nineteenth century has been a war on the able-bodied poor: an attempt to define, locate, and purge them from the rolls of relief."[12]

From the 1930s to the 1970s, liberals concentrated on assistance, creating programs designed to help the worthy poor and then adjusting them to dis-courage the able-bodied. Conservatives and the public complained about the fraud and abuse, but policymakers tended to focus much more on providing governmental assistance. Liberals debated how best to provide assistance and fought for increased benefit levels. In the 1980s, the focus turned more explic-itly toward personal responsibility, and conservatives entered the welfare pol-icy debate. By the 1990s, they dominated it.

In order to discourage individuals from seeking assistance, conservative ar-guments concentrated on the goals of *deterrence* and *rehabilitation*. Conserva-tives saw poverty not as a structural problem, but as a personal one. The theme of decentralization in the 1980s led to a renewed sense of individualism. Rather than the federal government taking responsibility for welfare, states, lo-calities, businesses, private charities, and individuals should address the prob-lems of poverty. Conservatives thought welfare recipients should be weaned off their reliance on government programs. There were two ways to do this. One was to use the concept of deterrence: Make welfare so difficult or undesir-able that fewer people would be inclined to apply for benefits. Thus, states in-troduced restrictive welfare programs: denying benefits to a woman who has more children while on welfare, whose children don't go to school, or who re-fuses to identify her children's father.[13] Another way to eliminate people from the welfare rolls was to rehabilitate the poor by giving them skills necessary to enter into the workforce. Requirements that welfare recipients work serve both to rehabilitate and to deter. If you are going to have to work in order to get your welfare grant, why not go out and get a job anyway? And if you do work while on welfare, you're gaining valuable experience that can help you get off.

Liberals and conservatives agreed that welfare recipients should be required to work. After all, liberals in the 1960s (as well as progressives in the early part of this century) were receptive to the idea of rehabilitation. But liberals in the

1960s talked about rehabilitation as a method of assisting the poor. In the 1990s, rehabilitation goes hand in hand with deterrence, and both are aimed at increasing personal responsibility. It seems that both welfare and welfare recipients are viewed as problems in the welfare debate. This viewpoint is criticized by liberals, who believe that much of the rhetoric around increasing personal responsibility reflects a willingness to blame the victim.

President Clinton himself contributed to the rightward shift of the welfare debate. As a centrist Democrat, he made a campaign promise to "end welfare as we know it." Many analysts believe that if he had acted on welfare first, before tackling health care, he would have had more success on both. Indeed, by deciding "to push his overhaul of health care above all [he] found himself derided as a big spending old Democrat and wound up being unable to get either proposal passed, even in a Democratic Congress."[14] As discussed in Chapter 3, after the dramatic failure of health care in Congress and the subsequent election of a Republican majority in both the House and Senate, Clinton's hands were tied in the area of welfare.

Even before the election of the Republican Congress, Clinton had moved to the right on welfare. One of his policy advisors, David T. Ellwood (now back at Harvard's Kennedy School of Government) proposed placing a time limit on welfare as a way to encourage recipients to work. Crucial to the time limit, according to Ellwood, was increased funding for services such as child care to assist welfare recipients in their transition to work. In Clinton's campaign book, *Putting People First,* he suggests not only requiring work after two years, he also advocates providing support through education, training, child care, and health care.[15] In addition, neither Ellwood nor Clinton intended to eliminate the entitlement status of welfare.[16]

However, once the Clinton administration proposed time-limiting welfare, it opened the door to conservatives who wanted to use the welfare system not only to encourage work, but also to discourage undesirable social behaviors. And conservatives in Congress also took advantage of the Clinton administration's charges that the welfare system was broken to bolster their case that its funding should be cut and that responsibility should be given back to the states. Essentially what happened is that Clinton, as a centrist Democrat, allowed Republicans to move further to the right in the welfare debate.[17] The Republican-controlled Congress boxed the president into a corner. He himself had said that welfare should be time-limited and that welfare reform was a high priority. Yet he twice vetoed Republican legislation in 1996—not over the issue of entitlement but over issues such as health care and child care. "He was seeking to take credit for a welfare revolution that he was simultaneously—and not altogether successfully—trying to rein in."[18] When Republicans called his bluff and removed the offending provisions, the president decided to sign the bill, consolidating the new conservative hold on welfare and doing what he said he would do in his 1992 campaign pledge—end welfare as we know it. Ironically, Clinton, by "establishing a national dialogue on welfare that put the issue on the political agenda," paved the way for a conservative "overhaul that was all but unimaginable during twelve years of Republican control of the White House."[19]

Critiques of Welfare As We Knew It

What was wrong with welfare as we knew it? This question reaches the heart of the welfare dilemma. After all, welfare itself was designed to alleviate the problem of poverty. Why is it that we now talk about the problems with welfare rather than the problem of poverty? The answer lies in the nature of the policymaking process. Chapter 3 demonstrated how the circular nature of the policy process often leads to incrementalism. That is, when we discover a program isn't working, we generally don't scrap it altogether but tinker with it around the edges. AFDC had been tinkered with since the 1930s, when it was instituted. The program had been with us so long we couldn't distinguish whether it contributed to or alleviated poverty. And, welfare is an easy target. Its constituents (the poor, young adults, and children) are not likely voters. Because Americans like to believe that everyone can rise to the top in the capitalistic system, they don't want to hear about those who are stuck at the bottom. Also, a program with as many rules and requirements as AFDC acquired over the last fifty years is bound to have its share of fraud and abuse.

There is no denying that welfare is viewed negatively by the public, has not eliminated the problem of poverty (although there are disagreements as to how much it has alleviated the problem), and is in need of some sort of change. Critics' charges against the welfare system as it existed prior to October 1996 generally fell into one of five categories:

1. The federal welfare system discouraged state innovation by not giving states enough flexibility in running their own programs.
2. It discouraged recipients from working.
3. It caused a breakdown of the family among low-income people.
4. It cost too much money.
5. It disproportionately harmed black families.

I shall address each in turn.

State Flexibility

In the colonial United States, local governments provided welfare to people who lived within their borders. The local nature of welfare stemmed from a sense of community: Neighbors helped provide for one another. The sense of community was heightened by the similar backgrounds of the colonists. By the late 1800s, problems with urban poor were exacerbated by cultural differences— those in poverty were immigrants or blacks. Welfare ceased being a local issue when the states stepped in to regulate welfare institutions, and it became a national issue when the states as well as the general public asked for assistance from the federal government. Even at the time of the New Deal, there was opposition to giving too much power over social policy to the federal government. By the time of the Great Society, a large number of people thought that the national government had taken on a role beyond its constitutionally mandated one. From the 1980s until today, there has been a movement to return to the states much of what is done at the national level—including provision of welfare policies.

State level officials, particularly governors, have long complained about the restrictive nature of federal welfare policy. The federal government, they say, has tied their hands with excessive regulations. By accepting federal funds for welfare, states must agree to administer it in compliance with federal law and must also agree to "match" federal spending with state dollars. Interestingly, current proponents of increased state authority are not suggesting the elimination of federal funding altogether. Reagan's "turnback" proposal would have had state governments take over AFDC entirely—including funding. That proved to be extremely unpopular with the states, which prefer to use federal money where possible, in an effort to keep state taxes lower. States would like to continue to receive the federal money, but they'd also like to have fewer strings attached to it.

Ever since the Reagan presidency, the states have had more and more opportunities to experiment with welfare. In the 1980s, President Reagan began issuing "waivers" from the rules of the welfare program to allow experimentation. Presidents Bush and Clinton also granted state waivers. Over the last few years, states have experimented with a variety of welfare initiatives, from instituting a "family cap" (cutting benefits to women who have more children while on welfare) to increasing transition benefits (receipt of Medicaid and child care benefits to allow former recipients to adjust to their new jobs). (See Table 4.1.) President Clinton has approved more waivers than the last two presidents combined. (See Table 4.2.) Remarkably, at the time of the passage of the PRWORA, twenty-five states already had waivers to end the entitlement status

TABLE 4.1　State Initiatives in Welfare Reform

Learnfare (School attendance requirements)
Bridefare
Family cap
Workfare
Time limits
Family planning mandates
Migration restrictions
Immunization requirements
Increases in transition benefits

SOURCE: Thomas Corbett, "Welfare Reform in Wisconsin: The Rhetoric and the Reality," Chapter 2 in Donald F. Norris and Lyke Thompson, eds., *The Politics of Welfare Reform* (London: Sage Publications, 1995); Jeffrey Henig, *Public Policy and Federalism: Issues in State and Local Politics* (New York: St. Martin's Press, 1985).

TABLE 4.2　President Clinton's Welfare Waivers

Waivers	Number of States
Time limits	17 states
Welfare-to-work, work requirements, or workfare	23 states
Require teenage mothers to live at home	25 states

SOURCE: Robert Pear, "A Welfare Revolution Hits Home, But Quietly," *New York Times*, August 13, 1995, p. A5.

of welfare; five more had waivers pending.[20] States complained about the waiver process, which involves submitting an application to the federal government describing the proposed program and waiting for federal approval. Instead of having to request waivers, state officials said, why not make the rules flexible enough so that states can be innovative?

Liberal arguments against state flexibility generally center around the concept of equality. If welfare were to be entirely a state function, then some states would have more extensive benefits than others, creating unequal treatment of the poor among the states. Even under AFDC, with more federal control of welfare, the states were left to determine benefit levels. And these levels varied widely, from a low of $120 per month in Mississippi to a high of $923 per month in Alaska. (See Table 4.3.) With increased flexibility, some states will have more restrictive requirements than others, cutting off benefits to women who have more children while on welfare, for example. Opponents of state flexibility see a "race to the bottom" at the state level—states creating more and more restrictive programs, spending less and less money, and eliminating more and more people from the welfare rolls.

TABLE 4.3 AFDC Maximum Benefit for a 3-person Family by State, 1994

State	Maximum Benefit
Alabama	$164
Alaska	923
Arizona	347
Arkansas	204
California	607
Colorado	356
Connecticut	680
Delaware	338
District of Columbia	409
Florida	303
Georgia	280
Hawaii	712
Idaho	317
Illinois	367
Indiana	288
Iowa	426
Kansas	429
Kentucky	228
Louisiana	190
Maine	418
Maryland	366
Massachusetts	579
Michigan (Wayne County)	459
Minnesota	532
Mississippi	120
Missouri	292
Montana	401
Nebraska	364
Nevada	348
New Hampshire	580
New Jersey	424
New Mexico	357
New York	577
North Carolina	272
North Dakota	409

(continues)

TABLE 4.3   *(continued)*

State	Maximum Benefit
Ohio	341
Oklahoma	324
Oregon	460
Pennsylvania	421
Rhode Island	554
South Carolina	200
South Dakota	417
Tennessee	185
Texas	184
Utah	414
Vermont	638
Virginia	354
Washington	546
West Virginia	249
Wisconsin	517
Wyoming	360
Guam	330
Puerto Rico	180
Virgin Islands	240
Median	366

SOURCE: U.S. Congress, House Committee on Ways and Means, *Overview of Entitlement Programs: 1994 Greenbook,* section 10, Table 10-2.

But the debate today does not revolve around providing assistance, it revolves around increasing personal responsibility. Thus, the moral argument for state flexibility comes in. It is natural and proper that states have their own welfare rules, benefit levels, and cutoff points because, as the Republican governors are fond of saying about social policy, "one size does not fit all." State flexibility means that the states can best determine how their welfare programs should be run.

Encouraging Work

According to the new consensus on welfare, the best way to reduce dependency is to move people from welfare to work, having them look for jobs as soon as they begin receiving benefits. The welfare system as it existed under AFDC had several problems with it that actually discouraged people from working. First, the primary way to qualify for welfare has been by being a single parent. Single parents face the problem of paying for care of their children while they work. Most of the jobs that a welfare client would be qualified for would not pay enough to cover child care costs. Second, as a welfare recipient works and earns money, that money both reduces the amount of the welfare grant and is subject to income tax (whereas welfare payments are not). A person on welfare who works may actually decrease the amount of money available to her family. Not surprisingly, the "working poor" (those whose work does not bring them above the poverty level but who are not on welfare) resent the fact that other individuals are getting federal checks without working. And in a society based on the work ethic, this resentment spreads to other groups as well. The expression, "a hand, not a handout" implied that public assistance was meant to be temporary, not an extended means of income. Public opinion today sees welfare as a handout to the undeserving poor, in contrast to the 1930s, when extended benefits to "worthy widows" were acceptable.

There are two ways to deal with the lack of work incentives in welfare. The first is to make work more attractive; the second is to make welfare less attractive. In the previous round of welfare reform (1988) the emphasis was on making work more attractive by providing assistance to welfare recipients in the form of increased child care and health care benefits, job training and placement assistance, and stipends for work-related expenses such as travel costs. This type of assistance can also cause resentment—why should welfare recipients have help in these areas when other working people do not? In addition, supportive services such as these cost money, driving up total spending on welfare. For these and other reasons, welfare reform is now based on the concept of deterrence, making welfare less attractive. Restrictions such as a family cap, requiring teenage mothers to live at home and provide the name of a child's father, or cutting benefits to parents whose children are truant are all means of deterring an individual from receiving welfare. Finally, time-limiting welfare, as was done in TANF—setting a limit of two years after which the primary caregiver is required to work and an overall lifetime limit of five years for receipt of welfare—is another way to encourage welfare families to work.

Deterring people from welfare by creating restrictions or time-limiting benefits was, until recently, a controversial issue. Although it is true that most welfare recipients are not working (see Table 4.4), it is not clear whether welfare has caused their unemployment or their unemployment has caused their need for welfare. There are two problems associated with work and welfare: job availability and job readiness. Many people are concerned about whether there are enough jobs available for the welfare recipients who will soon be asked to work in exchange for their benefits. When millions of current welfare recipients are forced into the job market, will they displace current workers? If they

TABLE 4.4　Percentage of AFDC Families with Earned Income, selected years

	Percentage of Families Headed by Mother	Percentage of Families Headed by Father
1986	6.2	1.0
1988	7.0	1.1
1990	6.9	1.1
1991	6.7	1.1
1992	6.1	1.1

SOURCE: U.S. Congress, House Committee on Ways and Means, *Overview of Entitlement Programs: 1994 Greenbook,* section 10, Table 10-29.

are unable to find jobs, will they end up homeless and destitute? Or will the labor market be able to absorb the newly independent welfare recipients? As one welfare policy analyst put it, "It's not like America needs 5 million single mothers looking for work at the low end of the labor market."[21]

One way to deal with a lack of available jobs is to create community service work for welfare recipients. Such a program requires an individual to work for her benefits, usually by dividing the benefit amount by the minimum wage to determine the number of hours to be worked. Individuals then can do work for the community, such as cleaning public parks, doing clerical work in government agencies, or even working for private businesses for a wage that is at least partially subsidized by the government. The advantage of workfare is that it removes (at least somewhat) the stigma attached to welfare; a person isn't receiving a handout but is working in exchange for benefits. In addition, that person is also getting valuable job experience.

Unfortunately, workfare also has problems, the greatest of which is its cost. Finding or creating jobs requires extra work for administrators, as does figuring out the amount of hours to be worked and checking to make sure that requirements are met. And, as difficult as it may be to believe, workfare programs have often had difficulty finding enough activities to keep the welfare recipients busy. Some private companies are unwilling to participate, due to union rules and the possibility of displacing other workers,[22] as well as fears that the welfare clients will not be as capable of job performance.

> Workfare jobs are problematic. They are costly in that work-related expenses, administration, and child care have to be paid in addition to welfare—the Congressional Budget Office estimates are $6,300 per recipient in addition to the welfare grant—and they displace regular employees.[23]

When President Clinton signed the welfare legislation, he challenged "every employer that ever made a disparaging remark about the welfare system" to consider hiring a welfare client. But it is not always easy for welfare clients to fit into the structured environment of a job. Using private companies to provide work for welfare recipients has proven difficult.

> Business people are frustrated by many welfare veterans. Many among those hired, while the most qualified of those screened, have problems that include absenteeism, lack of discipline about work hours, poor reading and communications skills, and open resentment when given direction. And the current programs have not even reached people on welfare who have more serious problems, like alcohol and drug abuse or low intelligence.[24]

In the 1980s, when the last welfare reform bill was passed, conservatives and liberals agreed that encouraging work should be a primary goal of any reform effort. The consensus was based in part on research performed by the Manpower Demonstration Research Corporation. In the early 1980s, states began experimenting with work and training programs, and the MDRC conducted a five-year study of eight states starting in 1982. Results of the study indicated that a small percentage of welfare recipients can be moved off of welfare permanently through work and training programs.[25] Conservatives and liberals agreed that welfare clients should receive some assistance designed to help them find and keep jobs, including work training, education, job placement services, and payment of child care and transportation costs. Clinton's Work and Responsibility Act (WRA), introduced in 1994, included increased funding for such assistance.

Family Breakdown

One of the biggest issues in welfare is the concept of family values. Many people believe that AFDC encouraged negative social behavior, most notably teenage pregnancy and single parenthood. Because AFDC had its origins in state mothers' aid programs, it started out explicitly for single mothers. In its early days, states often instituted "suitable home" provisions for AFDC families, which required that the single parent be a widow rather than divorced, "deserted" (meaning that the husband had left without getting a divorce), or never-married. During the 1950s and 1960s, the federal government cracked down on suitable home provisions, which in many instances were used to deny benefits to racial minorities. Suitable home provisions have been eliminated entirely. "The typical AFDC parent today is not the 'worthy widow' envisaged in the original legislation, but a divorced, deserted, or never-married woman."[26] Indeed, the number of single-parent families on welfare is quite high, as Table 4.5 illustrates. Welfare has never been directed at intact poor

TABLE 4.5   AFDC Characteristics

Year	1969	1979	1992
Average family size	4	3.6	2.9
Percent of families in which			
Parents divorced	43.3	44.7	30.0
No marriage	27.9	37.8	53.1
Teenaged mother	6.6	4.1	7.6
Caretaker is white	N/A	40.4	38.9
Caretaker is black	45.2	43.1	37.2
Caretaker is Hispanic	N/A	13.6	17.8

SOURCE: U.S. Congress, House Committee on Ways and Means, *Overview of Entitlement Programs: 1994 Greenbook,* section 10, Table 10-27.

families, simply because the original assumption was that in a two-parent family the father could work. As the rate of out-of-wedlock births soared in the 1970s, 1980s, and 1990s (among poor and nonpoor, white and minorities), welfare reflected a national trend. But while welfare still discouraged mothers from working, the numbers of women (including single mothers) in the workforce rapidly increased throughout the period. And by the 1990s, a program designed to give aid based on single parenthood while discouraging work seemed ludicrous. Even if AFDC did not create the problem, it certainly didn't discourage it.

In the 1992 presidential campaign, Vice President Dan Quayle hit a raw nerve when he criticized television character Murphy Brown for having a baby without getting married. Single mothers of all income levels were hurt by the implication that somehow they were responsible for the moral breakdown of society. And yet, many Americans longed for a time long gone (if it ever existed) when children grew up with both parents and neighbors took responsibility for neighborhood children.[27] At about the same time, news coverage of "deadbeat dads" (absent fathers who refuse to pay child support) gave credence to the idea that children were getting hurt by the breakup of the traditional two-parent family. Although many people still have decidedly mixed feelings about single parenthood, there is an increased emphasis on encouraging family stability in the 1990s. AFDC was a prime example of a policy that seemed to discourage such stability. "We have entrenched poverty in America because we have allowed—even encouraged—the values of family and community to deteriorate among the poor."[28] (See Chapter 1 for a discussion of the debate on whether welfare causes women to have children out of wedlock.)

Welfare became the target for restrictive policies designed to encourage "socially acceptable" behaviors. States requesting waivers from the federal government for the welfare programs were increasingly likely to institute restrictions on behavior. Welfare had become a program based on rehabilitation as well as deterrence. If the old requirements encouraged single parenthood, teenage pregnancy, and lack of work initiative, why not create a program that encouraged social values? Again, these state reforms were an attempt to change individual behavior on the assumption that poverty was caused by individual failings and exacerbated by misguided government programs. If the existing welfare programs inculcated a culture of poverty, policymakers reasoned that they could restructure welfare programs to inculcate a culture of work and family values.

As we have seen, not everyone agrees that poverty is caused by individual problems or by government social policies. For those who believe poverty is a societal problem, attempts to control behavior by restrictive welfare policies are paternalistic at best and cruel at worst. Why should poor people be punished for undesirable behavior while the nonpoor are free to behave as they wish? It is not entirely clear whether the pathologies associated with welfare are a cause or an effect of poverty. Viewed as a structural problem, poverty can only be eradicated by increasing the income of the poor. According to this view, attempts at behavior modification only worsen the conditions of poverty, and cutting off "unworthy" adults only puts their children at risk. Previous attempts at rehabilitating the poor, including poorhouses, prohibition, the scientific charity movement, and Great Society programs, have had limited success. The whole idea of a "culture" of poverty seems to have racist and classist undertones. Since many of the people on welfare are minorities, there is a tendency for some middle-class Americans to have negative attitudes toward them. Even some of those who agree that there is at least some connection between culture and poverty are not entirely sold on the idea of restrictive welfare programs. They might argue that it is better to use a carrot than a stick to change behavior. Policymakers should reward "good" behavior rather than punishing "bad," or they should provide additional support, such as job training, child care, or education, to help people lift themselves out of poverty.

In the 1980s, the concept of a "social contract" with the poor became popular among academics and policymakers. The idea was that the poor could expect to receive assistance from the government, and in return, the government could expect those receiving assistance to contribute to society by working or providing a stable family environment. Welfare would become a system of mutual rights and obligations. Many of the state reforms in the 1990s were based on the social contract. Welfare recipients are now called "clients," and in many states, they must sign "personal responsibility agreements" in exchange for receiving welfare benefits.[29]

Cutting Spending

One complaint that has been lobbed frequently against the current welfare programs is that they cost too much. This complaint is related to the issues discussed previously: If welfare is discouraging work and encouraging family breakdown, then any amount we spend on it is too much. If we could put people to work or otherwise encourage acceptable social behaviors, then welfare might be worth its cost. And welfare as it currently exists is a program that involves national redistribution. Since it is paid for by federal taxes, people of higher income levels in one state are subsidizing not only people of lower income levels in their state, but in other states as well.

Reducing federal expenditures can be accomplished in several ways. First, the federal government could simply end its role in welfare, eliminating welfare funding altogether and allowing states to create and pay for whatever welfare systems they wish. This is what President Reagan suggested in his "turnback" proposal, but it is not politically feasible in the current political environment. Eliminating federal spending on welfare would cause large variations among states in terms of welfare spending. While some might spend generous amounts on welfare, others might devote limited resources to the program. In addition, many would argue that the federal government has some obligation to care for its least well-off citizens, that this responsibility should not be left to the states alone. Although these arguments might have held sway a few years ago, they are not the major reason why we're not discussing eliminating federal spending on welfare. State governments, which are asking the federal government to reduce its requirements for welfare, are not asking to fund the system themselves since they would have to increase state taxes to do so, and they are already feeling a financial squeeze. They would much rather get federal money than have to tell their citizens they're raising taxes. State and local governments have always had to deal with the problem of poverty, and they would much rather have federal financial assistance to do what they would be doing anyway.

Another way to reduce spending is to *reduce* eligibility requirements. Making it easier to apply for benefits would actually save costs. Many of the costs of welfare are administrative. Every time a new requirement is added, administrative costs increase. The cheapest way to provide welfare would be to have something along the lines of a negative income tax through which people are given a check if they fall below a certain income level. This would drastically reduce administrative costs by basically eliminating the welfare bureaucracy. Of course, as we saw in Chapter 2, actually passing a law creating a negative income tax is not politically feasible.

Some of the methods that may reduce costs of welfare in the long run actually increase costs in the short run. Workfare is just one example. State initiatives that restrict eligibility may reduce costs in the long run by eliminating individuals from the welfare rolls, but they also increase costs in the short run by requiring more verification. These initiatives not only increase costs, but also enlarge the welfare bureaucracy. Any type of program encouraging work increases costs in the short run, not only due to more administrative costs, but also due to costs of training and child care. If these programs work, they eliminate people from the welfare rolls by giving them jobs, but again, those cost savings occur in the long run.

Democrats have criticized the TANF for eliminating people from the welfare rolls without making sufficient provision for those who have difficulty finding jobs. If welfare reform is successful and people find jobs, then costs will decrease. But if it is not successful and people are eliminated from the welfare rolls without jobs, then welfare costs may be decreased, but other costs may increase—homeless shelters and emergency and medical services will have to provide care for poor people who fall through the cracks. And even if governmental funding for all of these decreases, then private charities or individuals will have to take up the slack, still at a cost to society.

Welfare and Race

One difficult issue in welfare is the matter of race. The public perception is that most people on welfare are black, and this perception only adds to negative attitudes about welfare recipients. Discussions about an "underclass" that is not participating fully in society are often tinged with an element of racism: "Underclass" has become a code word for black, and some people use it to blame the poor (who are disproportionately black) for their own poverty. On the other hand, people who would like to reform the welfare system by encouraging work incentives are often unjustly accused of racism.

In 1965, Daniel Patrick Moynihan (now a Democratic senator from New York, then an advisor to President Johnson) authored a report about blacks and poverty called *The Negro Family: The Case for National Action,* in which he equated black poverty with the breakdown of inner-city families and a matriarchal society. In order to eliminate poverty, he said, the federal government must reinforce the family structure, which had been broken by the system of slavery and further hurt by migration to northern industrial cities. Out-of-wedlock births among blacks were high, and many families were headed by a female, with no adult male presence. This, he believed, led to a culture of poverty. Bring back stability to families, and the cycle of poverty could be broken.[30]

The "Moynihan Report" caused outrage among liberals, both black and white, who accused Moynihan of both racism and sexism. They were angry at him for implying that poverty was caused by personal failings and for his criticism of black family life. They felt his portrayal was paternalistic and condescending, and they were upset over his depiction of welfare as encouraging dependency. They also criticized his methodology. The report relied on anecdotes and did not provide sound theoretical support for his assertions. For his part, Moynihan, who had worked for both Presidents Kennedy and Johnson, retreated to academia, teaching at Harvard until he was offered a position as a domestic policy advisor in the Nixon White House. A lifelong Democrat, Moynihan decided to take the job both because he felt liberals in the Democratic party had betrayed him (the feeling was mutual) and because he hoped that conservatives could handle the welfare problem better. Once in the Nixon administration, he aligned himself with other liberals who were questioning the policy direction of Kennedy and Nixon. The group earned the name neoconservative.[31] Interestingly, although Moynihan was lambasted by liberals in the 1960s for his conservative opinions on welfare, as a Democratic senator in 1996, he took what had become the very liberal position of defending the entitlement status of welfare.

Moynihan's controversial thesis about the black family was revisited in 1987 with the publication of *The Truly Disadvantaged*, by William Julius Wilson, a black scholar now at Harvard University. Wilson argues that it is not so much racism as the structure of the economy that has kept a high proportion of blacks in poverty. Wilson blames the movement of jobs from the inner cities to the outlying suburbs for the persistent unemployment among black men. These high unemployment rates, according to Wilson, inhibit the rate of marriage in the inner city, creating a limited pool of men financially able to maintain and support a stable family. Black women thus have a difficult time finding suitable men to marry. The solution, according to Wilson, is to provide increased education, employment, and training to the "underclass" of black men in the inner cities.[32] Wilson's thesis—although still controversial—has been better received than Moynihan's. It has however, been criticized on several grounds: for ignoring the problems and accomplishments of black women[33] and for providing a justification for racist attacks against welfare.

The Personal Responsibility and Work Opportunity Reconciliation Act

The PRWORA was approved by large margins in both the House and Senate, despite the fact that many Democrats spoke out strongly against the bill. For

Speaker Newt Gingrich holds up a copy of the Contract with America as Republican Representatives look on. Photo courtesy of Corbis-Bettmann.

example, Senator Carol Moseley-Braun (D–IL) said that the Senate would "rue the day we passed this legislation," which she claimed would "do actual violence to poor children."[34] On the other side, Republican Representative Clay Shaw (FL) claimed that the bill would "rescue millions of Americans out of a corrupt welfare system."[35] Either way, the controversial legislation is obviously a major departure from the way welfare has been conducted in this country for the past sixty years. The Personal Responsibility and Work Opportunity Reconciliation Act has three main components: It ends the entitlement status of welfare; it gives welfare back to the states in the form of a block grant; and it emphasizes work (both by creating time limits and by instituting strict work requirements). The remainder of this section examines why those components have caused so much controversy.

Ending the Entitlement

The Personal Responsibility Act eliminates the entitlement status of welfare, creating in its place a new block grant called Temporary Assistance for Needy Families (TANF). (TANF replaces the AFDC program.) Under the new law, spending is capped, and the states receive lump-sum payments rather than open-ended entitlement funding. The end of open-ended funding means that welfare spending will be reduced. The new legislation saves $55 billion over six years.

The entitlement status of welfare had been held sacrosanct by the Congress, the Supreme Court, and the agencies implementing welfare. As an entitlement, anyone who was eligible for AFDC could sue the government if they were denied benefits, and by law, funding would have to increase commensurately with the number of people eligible. The only way to change this entitlement to welfare benefits was to change the statutory law—which Congress did when it established TANF. Eliminating the welfare entitlement was the most fundamental change to the welfare law. Not only did it cap spending, but it brought an end to the federal responsibility for taking care of anyone who fell into poverty. It signaled a change in attitude about the causes of poverty. By saying that recipients are no longer entitled to welfare, Congress was also saying that individual lack of initiative is the root problem of poverty. Ending the entitlement status of welfare marked the end of an era. AFDC, a New Deal and Great Society program, had been discredited, and the era of big government was over.

To many people, this change is viewed as an incredible folly. According to Senator Moynihan, the law "is not 'welfare reform,' it is 'welfare repeal.' It is the first step in dismantling the social contract that has been in place in the United States at least since the 1930s."[36] Moynihan and others believe that the government is abdicating its responsibility to poor people and that the safety net has been pulled out from under thousands of people. But this is now the minority opinion. The majority in Congress and throughout the nation believe that the entitlement status of welfare caused the problem of dependency. By ending the entitlement that poor people have to welfare, Congress and the president believe that welfare recipients will be forced to become self-sufficient.

Is the end of the welfare entitlement a repudiation of Roosevelt's New Deal commitment to the poor? Well, yes and no. Roosevelt was fighting what he saw as a temporary problem, caused by an economic crisis. The relief programs he created for the working poor would eventually "wither away" as the economy grew stronger and increased the number of available jobs. Any residual problems not taken care of by social security or unemployment insurance, he thought, would be handled by the states. He explicitly said that the federal government "must and shall quit this business of relief" once the economic crisis was over. He himself was worried about dependence on relief, which he called a "narcotic, a subtle destroyer of the human spirit."[37] ADC was not a relief program but a way to take care of dependent widows, who could not be expected to work. Because widows and single mothers covered by the AFDC program in the 1980s and 1990s were expected to work, the program itself was not what Roosevelt had intended.

On the other hand, Roosevelt believed that the government had a commitment to take care of the less fortunate in society, that it was the economic system (not the poor themselves) that caused poverty, and that the poor had a right to a minimum standard of living.[38] And, although it is impossible to predict what Roosevelt would think of the current welfare system, it is clear that the policies he proposed started us on a path toward a more expansive welfare state and that in federalizing welfare—even if only temporarily—Roosevelt was part of a long trend that centralized governmental authority over welfare programs. The TANF reverses that trend.

Creating a Block Grant

In ending the federal guarantee of welfare, the PRWORA also created the Temporary Assistance for Needy Families block grant, a lump-sum payment the states will use to fund their own poverty assistance programs. Theoretically, block grants are less restrictive than categorical grants. The change will give states more flexibility to spend the federal money as they wish. However, the block grants do come with some restrictions. States are required to have mandatory work requirements for welfare clients. Most will be asked to work within two years of receiving benefits, and individuals will face a lifetime limit of five years for receipt of welfare. In addition, states are prohibited from giving food stamps and Supplemental Security Income to legal immigrants who are not yet citizens. (Illegal immigrants have long been ineligible for welfare benefits.) States are also required to make increased efforts to identify absent fathers and procure child support payments from them.

However, states are free to use the money to create restrictive welfare programs. For example, they may cut off benefits to mothers who have more children while on welfare or to parents whose children do not attend school regularly. Previously, states had to get permission from the federal government in the form of waivers from the rules of AFDC, and such permission was not always quick in coming. When Massachusetts passed a strict new welfare law in 1995, it required a total of more than one hundred telephone conferences between state administrators and federal officials from the Departments of Health and Human Services and Agriculture. Even after all that, the federal government would not let the state enact its toughest provision—limiting receipt of welfare to two years, even if the parent had not been able to find a job.[39] The new block grant eliminates the need for waivers. As long as states are following the basic requirements of the grant, they can make their programs as restrictive as they want, without having to get the consent of the federal government.

Block grants, by giving states more authority, also limit the federal government's responsibility. According to Anna Kondratas, a conservative analyst at the

Hudson Institute, "The welfare reform debate does not seem to be grappling with the issues of radical redesign of welfare policy. Block granting everything in sight [is] kicking the problem down to the states to solve."[40] This means that the states get both the credit for successful programs and the blame for unsuccessful ones.

Since President Nixon first began to use block grants as part of his new federalism, they have been popular with governors—especially Republican governors—who like the idea of more freedom in implementing policy and also the idea of saving state as well as federal money.[41] Over the next few years, funding for the block grants will decrease. The hope is that, with more welfare recipients in jobs, the states will need less money for their welfare programs. On the other hand, if it proves difficult to find jobs for welfare recipients or the welfare rolls increase due to a recession, then states will have to bear the burden more or less on their own. (The legislation does allow for increased funding under special circumstances.) In the future, the states will be the arena in which welfare policy is debated.

Emphasizing Work

The biggest change facing the states is the requirement that adults begin working within two years of receiving assistance. A single parent must work for at least twenty-five hours per week and at least one of the parents in a two-parent family must work thirty-five hours per week. The bill includes an "escape hatch" for states, exempting up to 20 percent of the recipients from the work requirements for hardship reasons.[42]

Even allowing for the hardship exemption, analysts fear that more than a million children may become poor because their parents have been stricken from the welfare rolls.[43] And it is not clear whether the labor market can absorb all the new job applicants. Even Lawrence Mead, a political scientist who has long advocated work requirements, says that we can't estimate how the labor market will react because it's unclear how many of the welfare mothers are employable. Nonetheless, he believes the market will absorb the new workers, at least in the long run. Others worry about how the former welfare recipients will fare once their benefits run out and they are working on their own. Gary Burtless, a senior fellow at the Brookings Institution, predicts that one-fourth of the welfare mothers will be able to maintain their jobs and earn at least as much as they did on welfare, one-half will be worse off than they were on welfare, and one-fourth will "be in such severe difficulty that they will have to give up their children, or in trying to keep their families together, they will spend time as homeless people."[44]

Proponents of the new requirements counter that the present system hasn't been working and that the time has come to try new ideas. William Bennett, Secretary of Education under Reagan and now an Olin fellow at the Heritage Foundation, offers an argument for the new legislation and an indictment of the old system:

> Can welfare reformers guarantee that fundamental reforms in welfare will not cause some dislocation and suffering? Of course not. But the relevant question is: compared to what? The burden of proof rests not on those who would try something new but on those who would defend the horrors of the status quo. After all, proponents of welfare reform can make a plausible case that the current system is exacting a far higher cost than what will replace it.[45]

Conclusion

Welfare policy has changed incrementally over the last sixty years, evolving from a mostly local function to a state-federal function, and then gradually devolving to the states. On the one hand, TANF is an abrupt departure from the past. By ending the entitlement status of welfare and changing the system from cash assistance to employment assistance, TANF fundamentally alters the theoretical underpinning of welfare. Welfare no longer simply provides aid to the poor; instead it requires the poor to take responsibility for themselves. Fighting poverty is now secondary to encouraging self-sufficiency. And the assumption that poverty is caused by structural problems in the economy has been replaced by the assumption that it is caused by individual failing and lack of personal initiative.

On the other hand, TANF is indeed an incremental change. Reagan first proposed giving welfare back to the states, and ever since, the federal government has been allowing—even encouraging—states to experiment with welfare. These experiments have involved work requirements, restrictions, and time limits, all of which are reflected in TANF. The welfare debate has shifted to the right, but that shift has been gradually occurring over the last twenty years or so. After all, it was a Democratic president who proposed time-limiting welfare and who ultimately signed the most conservative reform of welfare in sixty years. Can TANF end dependency and truly reform welfare? Only time will tell.

5

....

Implementation and Beyond: The Present and Future of Welfare Reform

This is not the end of welfare reform; this is the beginning.

President Clinton, on signing welfare reform,
August 22, 1996

Good legislation is about ten percent of what's required to achieve true welfare reform. The other 90 percent is implementation, and that's going to take a lot of cooperation between Democrats and Republicans in Congress.

Representative Clay Shaw, Chairman,
House Subcommittee on Human Resources,
September 1996

T he policymaking process is a circular one, with changes in policy begetting more changes in policy. Chapter 3 described the initial stages of the policy process: agenda-setting, policy formulation, and legitimation. This chapter discusses in greater detail the implementation of the new law; that is, how it will actually be administered at the state level. Under the Personal Responsibility and Work Opportunity Act (PRWORA), states have more flexibility in developing welfare programs, but they are required to submit "state plans" to the federal Department of Health and Human Services (HHS). As implementation progresses, it is likely that state and federal governments will discover problems with the legislation, and these problems will likely be addressed by amendments to the PRWORA or perhaps by regulations promulgated by HHS. States, the federal government, outside research organizations, and the general public will be watching carefully to see what happens under the new welfare law. As they assess its success, welfare reform enters the evaluation stage. And, as illustrated in Table 5.1, the evaluation stage eventually leads back to the agenda-setting stage as issues raised in evaluations give rise to calls for changes in law. Whether this process results in small, incremental changes or in yet another round of major reform remains to be seen.

In fact the PRWORA has already been amended. President Clinton, in making his decision to sign the Republican welfare reform bill, was advised that he could make changes to the provisions that he found most onerous after the 1996 election. Even at the Rose Garden ceremony at which he signed the bill, President Clinton promised that welfare reform was only just beginning. Later, in an effort to appease liberal Democrats, HHS Secretary Donna Shalala (who had advised the president not to sign the bill) made a vow to the Democratic National Convention in August 1996. "I promise you this, on behalf of the president: that this bill will be changed and that this bill will be improved in the years ahead until we get it right for American families."[1] The first of those changes occurred in the budget bill passed in the summer of 1997. Thus the PRWORA may be the end of welfare as we know it, but it is only the beginning of welfare reform.

TABLE 5.1   Welfare Reform: The Circular Nature of the Policy Process

Agenda-Setting	1992	Candidate Clinton calls for an end to welfare.
	1994	President Clinton's welfare reform plan dies in Congress.
		The Contract with America contains a welfare reform plank.
	1996	Presidential election campaign brings welfare reform to the forefront.
Formulation	1995	President Clinton vetoes congressional welfare reform as part of a deficit-reduction bill.
	1996	President Clinton vetoes welfare reform as a stand-alone measure.
Legitimation	1996	Republicans remove Medicaid provisions. Democrats agree to ending the entitlement. Welfare reform is considered in the House and Senate, sent to conference committee; conference version is approved by both houses.
		President Clinton signs welfare reform.
Implementation	October 1, 1996	AFDC ends and is replaced by the TANF block grant.
	August, 1996	Noncitizens lose benefits.
	October 1, 1996	Food stamps funding begins to decrease.
	July 1, 1997	States must submit new welfare reform plans to HHS.
Evaluation	1997–1998	As states begin to implement their plans, results begin to come in.
		Ongoing evaluations will undoubtedly lead back to agenda-setting, as new problems become evident.

Welfare Reform Legislation

Provisions

Getting welfare reform passed in Congress, as difficult as that was, is only part of the story. The PRWORA sets in motion a series of changes that impact state and local governments as well as individuals and families. The broad-scale legislation affects social spending in a variety of areas. Under the PRWORA, Aid to Families with Dependent Children (AFDC), which had been known as the federal welfare program, is eliminated and replaced with Temporary Assistance for Needy Families (TANF), a block grant. In addition, as shown in Table 5.2, the act makes changes to Supplemental Security Income (assistance to low-income aged, blind, and disabled, including children), child support enforcement (the method by which the government attempts to establish paternity and enforce child support orders), the eligibility of immigrants for federal benefits, child protection programs (including adoption and foster care programs), child care funding, child nutrition programs (including school breakfast programs and food programs for pregnant women and infants), and the food stamp program (vouchers to qualified individuals to purchase food). The law is expected to save $54.6 billion over five years, mostly by cutting spending in the food stamp program and by denying food stamps and other benefits to legal immigrants.

The law also has an "escape hatch" in case the economy weakens. States with high unemployment will be eligible to receive money from a rainy day fund of $2 billion. In addition, states that are successful in meeting the goal of moving recipients into work will be eligible for money from a $1 billion bonus fund.

Block Grant Funding and Work Requirements

The widespread changes required by the act take place over an extended time period. Although the act ended the entitlement status of welfare as of October 1, 1996, when the TANF block grant went into effect, many parts of the act will be phased in gradually until 2002. And for the forty-three states that had waivers approved prior to passage of the act, some of the requirements may not apply until the waivers expire (anywhere from five to eleven years from now). Interestingly, despite the sweeping changes mandated by the law and dire predictions from Democrats such as Senator Moynihan, much of the impact of the act will not be felt for some time. There are two reasons for this. First, although overall spending on welfare will be reduced by 2002, states will actually receive more funding under the TANF block grant than they would have under AFDC during the first two years of the program. This is because block grant funding is based on the number of people each state had on the welfare rolls in 1995, and the rolls have been dropping since then. Thus, there were fewer people on welfare in 1997, even before PRWORA went into effect, than there had been two years earlier. The caveat is that the total amount of the block grant, $16.4 billion, will remain the same until 2002. It will not be ad-

TABLE 5.2   Major Provisions of PRWORA

Welfare
Ends the federal guarantee of providing welfare checks to all eligible families; allows states to create their own welfare programs, imposes work requirements, and creates a lifetime limit of five years for receipt of benefits. Replaces Aid to Families with Dependent Children (AFDC) with Temporary Assistance for Needy Families (TANF).

Supplemental Security Income
Changes the eligibility requirements for children, making it more difficult to qualify for benefits. The Congressional Budget Office estimates that about 22% of children who would have qualified for SSI under the old rules will lose eligibility by 2002.

Child Support Enforcement
Requires states to set up registries to track the status of child support orders; gives child support money collected by the state directly to welfare families, rather than using it to reimburse state expenses. Makes it easier for states to establish paternity.

Immigration
Makes legal immigrants ineligible for SSI and food stamps unless they become citizens. Exempts refugees and those granted asylum, as well as those who have worked in the United States for ten years or more. (Much of the reduction in spending comes from cuts in benefits to immigrants and cuts in food stamp spending.)

Child Protection
Makes minor changes to child protection (adoption and foster care) programs; maintains their current structure.

Child Care
Revises the existing block grant under which child care funds are provided to the states.

Child Nutrition
Retains the existing structure of most child nutrition programs, while limiting spending on summer food service and school breakfasts, child and adult care food program, and WIC (Women, Infants, and Children, a nutrition program for pregnant women, infants, and young children).

Food Stamps
Maintains the structure of the program, while reducing the benefits that eligible recipients qualify for. Requires able-bodied food stamp recipients between 18 and 50 to work or face cut-off of benefits.

Other Provisions
HHS secretary is required to implement a plan to prevent out-of-wedlock teen pregnancies; reduces social services block grant spending; scales back the Earned-Income Tax Credit (which provides tax benefits to low-income workers); sets aside $50 million for education to promote abstinence from sexual activity.

SOURCE: Jeffrey Katz, "Provisions: Welfare Overhaul Law," *Congressional Quarterly Weekly Report,* September 21, 1996, pp. 2696–2705.

justed for inflation, population growth, or any increases in the welfare rolls.[2] So although states may get increased funding for the first two years of implementation, that amount will remain constant for a few more years. What seems like a large amount of money today may not seem so large two or three years down the road.

The second reason that the impact of welfare reform will not immediately be felt has to do with the phase-in of the work requirements, as well as exemptions from them. One of the distinguishing features of the new welfare reform law is that it requires welfare recipients to begin working within two years of receiving aid. States who don't meet the work requirement could have their block grant reduced by 5 percent in the first year; that amount rises to a maximum deduction of 21 percent after the third year of implementation.

However, for the first couple of years of the program, "participation rates" (the percentage of people on welfare in a state who must be "participating" in the work requirements) may be 15 percent or less of the welfare caseload in many states. That is, the federal government will consider states to be complying with the work requirements even if only a small portion of people receiving benefits are actually working within two years of receiving aid. How can this be? First, like the penalties, the participation rates start small and gradually increase. By the year 2002, 50 percent of a state's welfare caseload is expected to be working. But in 1997, only 25 percent of the people receiving benefits are expected to work. As shown in Table 5.3, that percentage increases gradually over several years.

In addition, the law gives exemptions from the work requirement to states that have reduced caseloads. That is, if the number of welfare recipients in a state has decreased since 1995, the state's work requirement is reduced. For example, if a state's caseload as of 1997 is down 10 percent from 1995, that state's 1997 participation rate of 25 percent is reduced to 15 percent. Thus, a state may be required to put only a very small portion of its welfare population to work in the early years of the program.[3] This "caseload-reduction credit" rewards states for having smaller numbers of people on welfare. Most states will get the credit since, as noted previously, in most states the welfare caseload has been going down. Liberals complain that, combined with the end of the entitlement to welfare, the caseload-reduction credit encourages states to throw families off of welfare.

Caseload Reductions

The reduction in caseloads is a story unto itself. Between 1994 and 1996, the number of families on welfare nationwide dropped by about 14 percent, with

TABLE 5.3   Work Participation Rates Under TANF

Fiscal Year	Percent of Caseload Expected to Work
1997	25
1998	30
1999	35
2000	40
2001	45
2002 (and thereafter)	50

some states having even larger reductions (Maryland and Wisconsin saw drops in caseloads of 26 and 24 percent, respectively).[4] The drop began and was noticed before the PRWORA was even signed. Both Democrats and Republicans sought to take credit for the drop in caseloads, which they believed symbolized a reduction in dependency on welfare. Noting that caseload reduction started after Clinton had taken office, Clinton advisors used it as a campaign issue, claiming the change as a presidential success, whereas congressional Republicans said that it demonstrated the effectiveness of Republican welfare plans at the state level.[5] In reality, no one knows for certain what caused the decline in caseloads, but researchers attribute it to a variety of factors. Perhaps the most important factor is a strong economy, which means that more people are employed and thus fewer people find welfare necessary. But the economy alone is not a sufficient explanation. State welfare reform initiatives (implemented prior to the PRWORA under the waiver process) also had an impact on the decline in caseloads. These initiatives often entailed aggressive efforts to put welfare recipients to work and also restricted eligibility requirements, making fewer people eligible for welfare in the first place. In addition, the changed political environment surrounding welfare probably discouraged eligible individuals from applying. According to political scientist James Q. Wilson, "The stigma has been reattached to welfare. That will affect the behavior of some people, perhaps a lot of people."[6]

The reductions in caseloads, although not a direct result of the PRWORA (since they started occurring before it was enacted), are a result of the new political climate in which the PRWORA was passed. In fact, most of the decline took place between 1994 and 1996, when efforts by Congress and the president were making "ending welfare as we know it" headline news.[7] The climate in most states has meant that individuals are encouraged to find work instead of going on welfare, and even those who apply for welfare are expected to work. Restrictions on welfare have made fewer people eligible, and overall, the restrictions and expectations have made welfare less desirable, and perhaps, as Wilson suggests, they have reinforced the stigma attached to welfare. Deterrence, combined with a strong economy, seems to be working, inasmuch as there are fewer people on welfare. What happens to those people who have left welfare is another question. "The Republicans who devised the caseload reduction credit acknowledge that they do not know what happens to all the parents and children leaving the welfare rolls. Democrats say many of those families sink deeper into poverty. Republicans say the adults will find jobs and will ultimately be better off."[8] This is one question that will certainly be examined in the evaluation process.

Implementation Issues

Shake-up at HHS

Even before implementation of the PRWORA began, problems emerged. First, some administration officials in the Department of Health and Human Services, which has overall responsibility for welfare, balked at having to implement a law that they found objectionable. The first to announce his resignation was economist Wendell Primus, who made his announcement even before President Clinton signed the bill. In his letter of resignation, dated August 17, 1996, Primus said:

> I believe strongly that a political appointee must be able to support the Administration's policies that fall under his purview. Given the president's decision to sign the welfare reform bill, I have no choice but to resign. To remain would be to disown all the analysis my office has produced regarding the impact of the bill.[9]

Primus, who had been deputy assistant secretary of planning and evaluation in HHS, helped produce a study estimating that large numbers of children would be put into poverty under the bill that President Clinton vetoed in late 1995 and early 1996. Previous to working in the Clinton administration, Primus had been chief of staff of the human resources subcommittee of the Ways and Means Committee in the Democratic Congress.

On September 11, Assistant Secretaries Mary Jo Bane and Peter Edelman, two of the most senior officials on welfare policy, announced that they too would be leaving because of their opposition to the new law. Bane sent her staff an e-mail expressing her "deep concerns" about the welfare bill, saying the concerns "have led me to conclude that I cannot continue to serve" in the Clinton administration. Edelman said in a memo to his staff, "I have devoted the last 30-plus years to doing whatever I could to help in reducing poverty in America. I believe the recently enacted welfare bill goes in the opposite direction."[10] Edelman's wife

Marian Wright Edelman, a close friend of Hillary Rodham Clinton, directs the Children's Defense Fund, which had lobbied extensively against the legislation. Peter Edelman had replaced David T. Ellwood, who had resigned a year earlier in protest of the administration's willingness to end the entitlement status of welfare.[11] Despite the fact that she opposed the bill, HHS Secretary Donna Shalala announced that she would stay on for Clinton's second term.

State Concerns

Administration shake-ups are relatively common as a president moves into his second term, although officials do not usually specify a single policy as the reason for their departure. But even as the administration was adjusting to the resignations, states too began to get nervous about implementing the new block grant. State officials were most concerned about vague language in the new law and fearful of interpreting provisions differently from the administration. For example, the PRWORA says that states must "guarantee fair and equitable treatment of beneficiaries," without specifying what constitutes fairness and equity. Under old AFDC rules, states had specific eligibility requirements to follow. Under TANF, states are given flexibility to determine eligibility, but state officials fear that the federal government may interpret their new requirements to be unfair or inequitable. In addition, states complained about language exempting recipients with children under six years of age from the work requirements if they cannot find "appropriate child care." Who is to determine the appropriateness of child care, states wanted to know. States, the federal government, the mothers? State welfare officials brought these and other questions to federal officials, asking for more guidance in implementing the new law. The irony of state officials asking for more guidance after years of begging for more flexibility was not lost on federal officials. After a meeting between federal and state welfare administrators in September 1996, one administration official commented, "States are like the dog that ran after the car and finally caught it. Now they're not sure what to do with it. It's amazing what happens when you actually get something you wish for."[12] For their part, Republicans in Congress dismissed the governors' complaints. According to House Budget Committee Chairman John Kasich:

> It is not unexpected for governors to say, "Oh, woe is me, look how tough this is going to be." The governors are trying to make sure they can do the best they can to get as much money . . . back to their states. I think the governors ought to just stop bellyaching because we gave them a great opportunity to participate in this and, frankly, I'm interested in them doing their job and get on with it.[13]

Interestingly, as states began to develop their state plans for using the TANF money, most did not take advantage of the opportunity to completely overhaul welfare, by lowering benefits to recipients, for example, or stopping the issuance of welfare checks altogether. California's state plan simply continued its AFDC program. Some states imposed stricter time limits.[14] States appeared more concerned about complying with new federal requirements than with creating innovative programs. For example, although the lifetime limit of five years will not affect states until 2001, states began to worry early on about how to enforce the new rule. (The clock for the lifetime limits began ticking on October 1, 1996, when TANF went into effect; a family that had been on AFDC for years previous to that time would have five years from 1996 before they would be removed from TANF.) Most states did not keep track of how long AFDC recipients received welfare. States were concerned about how to develop computer systems to keep track of such information and about how they would exchange that information with each other.[15]

Clinton Administration Proposals

Shortly after the election, Clinton administration officials announced that they were developing legislative proposals to revise the welfare law, adjusting some of the provisions that Democrats found most onerous. The administration offered three proposals. The first would reinstate food stamp eligibility for legal aliens; the second would increase food stamp benefits for families with high housing costs; and the third would relax the work requirements under the food stamps provision. In total, these revisions would restore about $14 billion in spending on welfare over six years. Liberal interest groups such as the Food Research and Action Center and the Center on Budget and Policy Priorities supported the changes. Congressional Republicans, however, were not pleased with the administration proposals, saying that Clinton was attempting to change the substance of the bill that he had signed. Clay Shaw, chair of the Human Resources Subcommittee in the House, responded to the Clinton proposals: "There will be some technical corrections. But any substantive change in the law would certainly be rejected at this time. There's no sense changing it before you give it a chance to work."[16]

Democrats in Congress agreed. Senate Minority Leader Tom Daschle (who voted against PRWORA) said that Clinton should allow the states to begin implementation before instituting changes in the law, noting that the political climate in Congress was not open to legislative tinkering.[17] Not only Republicans were resentful of Clinton's attempts to alter welfare reform; so too were liberal

Democrats, who were furious with the president for signing the bill in the first place and who were not inclined to extend him any legislative favors.

Pete Stark (D–CA) criticized the proposals to soften the law: "The president sold out children to get re-elected. He's no better than the Republicans." Representative Stark, reflecting the view of liberals in Congress, said, "We thought it was wrongheaded to begin with, when the Republicans proposed it, and it was a sellout by the president to sign it."[18] Eventually, however, Congressional Democrats and Republicans relented and the Balanced Budget Act (BBA) of 1997 included some changes to the welfare law.

The Dilemma Revisited

This book examines the main dilemma of welfare reform: Can we help those in poverty without causing dependence on government programs? At various times in U.S. history, we have seen assistance to those in poverty as the main goal of welfare; the political climate now emphasizes reducing dependence as the primary aim of government policy. Let us now revisit that dilemma in the context of the 1996 reform. Several themes related to the dilemma have been presented throughout the book: the tension between individualism and community in the United States; the competing goals of prevention, rehabilitation, assistance, and deterrence; the incremental nature of policy change; and the conflict between ideological purity and politics. This section examines how each of these themes has been addressed by the latest round of welfare reform.

Individualism Versus Community

America has a long history of "rugged individualism," a pioneer spirit that emphasizes the ability of each individual to take care of himself or herself through perseverance and hard work. Individualism implies that the poor, like everybody else, should take care of themselves. Making it too easy to receive assistance only weakens the can-do spirit that American political culture encourages. On the other hand, the United States also has a history of community, a sense that individuals should not just care for themselves, but for each other. This feeling of community means that most Americans feel an obligation to care for those who are undergoing hard times. Thus, the public expected the government to provide assistance to help the public cope with the depression. More often, however, it is difficult to decide where community ends and individualism begins. One way that we can reconcile the competing interests of community and individualism is by making sure that assistance goes only to the "worthy" poor, who deserve our help, forcing others to rely on themselves. Unfortunately, definitions of who is worthy and unworthy often become intertwined with fear of differences, so that those who are different because of race or ethnicity or religion seem to be the easiest to classify as unworthy.

Currently, the United States is not in a period of economic crisis, and individualism seems to be the guiding force behind the new welfare law. Although assistance will still be provided to the poor, that assistance is temporary—lasting only five years for any one family, and conditional—requiring that adult welfare recipients find jobs and otherwise change their behavior. When it comes to welfare, it seems that our sense of community has been spent. Public opinion currently favors a get-tough attitude toward welfare, an attitude reinforced by our reliance on individualism.

Deterrence, Rehabilitation, Prevention, and Assistance

Any attempt at providing welfare can do one or a combination of four things: It can assist the poor by simply providing them with money or goods; it can prevent poverty by making structural changes to the economy; it can deter individuals from seeking aid by making it undesirable; or it can seek to rehabilitate individuals, changing their behavior so that they can bring themselves out of poverty.

In keeping with our current emphasis on individualism, the 1996 welfare law embodies a combination of deterrence and rehabilitation. Since welfare recipients face a lifetime limit, work requirements, and a renewed stigma attached to receiving welfare, the expectation is that they will be deterred from applying for it in the first place. This "tough-love" attitude is also supposed to rehabilitate welfare recipients, who will face new expectations about finding and keeping jobs. Proponents of the new law argue that it will, in the long run, assist the poor, by giving them incentives to work, and prevent poverty, by making work more desirable than welfare. Opponents argue that the law does not assist the poor but rather punishes them for their poverty. They believe that many of the poor who are not working have legitimate problems finding jobs and paying for day care and health care, problems for which they need assistance, not deterrence.

Incremental Change Versus Comprehensive Change

For most of its history, changes in welfare law have been incremental. That is, change has occurred a little bit at a time, leaving us with a piecemeal system that has perverse incentives and requirements that no longer seem reasonable. Modifications have been made by tinkering around the edges, rather than by reexamining underlying assumptions. The PRWORA changed all that. Unlike all past reforms of welfare, it is comprehensive and rational rather than piecemeal and incremental. Reformers started by changing the tenets of welfare and then changed policy to reflect the new principles. In this sense, welfare reform in 1996 was a truly historic event.

On the other hand, there were some incremental elements to the new law. The idea of replacing AFDC with a block grant had been originally proposed by Ronald Reagan in the 1980s. And although the idea of giving welfare to the states is a landmark change, the states had in fact already been trying out a variety of innovative new welfare laws under the waiver process. Thus, the monumental change in welfare started out as a gradual process. What is most significant is that welfare reformers in 1996 started from scratch, throwing out the old program (AFDC) and instituting a new one (TANF). This type of change does not occur often. Presumably, future changes to TANF will be incremental rather than comprehensive, as policymakers attempt to fine-tune problems with the legislation.

Ideological Purity Versus Political Gain

In this particular arena, Republicans were the winners in 1996. Although they made compromises (a necessary part of any legislation), the Republicans maintained their overall commitment to the welfare reform plan outlined in the Contract with America. There were some moments in 1996 when Republicans appeared willing to stall their own reform plan in order to make the president look bad. However, they ultimately decided that they could serve their own ideology and gain political advantage by passing welfare reform. Democrats, for the most part, had a more difficult time with welfare reform. Few Democrats would have suggested ending the entitlement status of welfare, and few initially favored the Republican reform plan. But faced with grim reelection prospects and a president who had decided to sign the Republican bill, many Democrats voted with public opinion rather than their own party's ideology. The president, who faced the prospect of reneging on his promise to end welfare, ultimately signed legislation that he did not like and that his cabinet advised him to veto. Sometimes the political process creates difficult choices, and this was one of those times for Democrats. Most (with some notable exceptions) seemed to go with their political rather than their ideological instincts.

Conclusion

If previous history is any guide, the latest attempt at welfare reform will only spawn new attempts to change the system. The United States has moved from an individual interpretation of poverty to a structural interpretation and then back again. Welfare has evolved from a local to a state and then to a federal-state and federal-local function, and now it is devolving back to a state function. As long as there are poor people in this country (and there is no reason to reasonably expect that we can make poverty disappear), the United States will always have a difficult time determining what to do about them. We are torn between our desire to help the poor out of a feeling of community with them, and our faith in individualism, capitalism, and hard work as the keys for people helping themselves. We are not sure whether the poor are worthy or unworthy of our assistance. And we have a great deal of difficulty determining the difference.

However, with passage of the new law, we can no longer blame poverty on welfare. We have decided that reducing dependency is our ultimate goal in welfare. Will that help the poor? That remains to be seen. But with AFDC and its entitlement abolished, welfare can no longer be said to be the problem. Dependence has been legislated out of existence. If poverty persists, then new attempts at reform will have to acknowledge that poverty is the problem.

No one can predict unequivocally what the consequences of the new welfare law will be. It was clear that something needed to be done; action rather than talk in welfare reform has been long in coming. William Bennett expressed this need to act just prior to President Clinton's signing of the PRWORA in August of 1996:

> There is now a powerful consensus that the welfare system is ruinous and fundamentally flawed. At the same time, there are different, compelling, but mostly untried theories about what ought to replace it. It is now time to try them. . . .
>
> Breaking the cycle of illegitimacy and dependency ultimately depends on stopping widespread, deeply entrenched, and highly destructive behavior. This will not be easy; there are a number of noneconomic cultural forces at work. Policy reforms alone are not sufficient to the task. But they are necessary.[19]

Necessary as they may be, policy reforms are not infallible. We should learn from the lessons of welfare reform past and present as we embark on our latest attempt to end welfare as we know it.

Discussion Questions

Chapter 1

1. Define the word "welfare." How does its common usage differ from the dictionary definition?

2. What is meant by the distinction between "worthy" and "unworthy" poor?

3. What are some of the myths about welfare? Why do you think they have been so persistent?

4. Explain why some people believe that welfare programs cause dependence. Do you agree or disagree?

Chapter 2

1. How and why does U.S. welfare policy reflect values from Elizabethan England?

2. What are the four goals of welfare policy?

3. Explain how individualism and the Protestant work ethic have impacted welfare policy in the United States.

4. How did the immigrant population impact poverty policy?

5. What were some of the similarities and differences between the New Deal and the Great Society?

Chapter 3

1. What are the stages in the policy process, and how does welfare fit into each?

2. What was the importance of Medicaid provisions in the passage of welfare legislation?

3. Why do you think President Clinton decided to sign the welfare bill?

4. Why was welfare considered an *entitlement* in the past?

5. What role did the 1996 election play in the passage of welfare reform?

Chapter 4

1. Discuss some of the problems with the *poverty line*.

2. Do you believe that poverty is caused by *individual* problems or by *structural* problems? Explain why.

3. How and why did the welfare debate move to the right?

4. Evaluate the three main goals of the Personal Responsibility and Work Opportunity Reconciliation Act.

Chapter 5

1. How would you define the goals for poverty policy in the United States?

2. Do you think politicians should take responsibility for problems in the implementation of the Personal Responsibility and Work Opportunity Reconciliation Act? Why or why not?

3. Do you believe that PRWORA will create a new, better society, less dependent on government programs, or is it taking away the safety net and paving the way for homelessness and increased poverty? Defend your view.

Glossary

AFDC (Aid to Families with Dependent Children) is the program that we used to refer to as "welfare." It provided cash grants to families with children who meet certain income and other requirements. The state had to contribute a specified sum of money for the program in addition to what the federal government contributed. AFDC, which was a categorical grant program, has been replaced by the TANF block grant under the Personal Responsibility and Work Opportunity Reconciliation Act.

Block grants are sums of money the federal government gives to the states to provide specified services (such as child care or medical care). Although the money must be used for its intended purpose, the state has some leeway as to how it may be spent. A block grant is a finite pool of money. In 1996, Congress passed legislation that abolished the former AFDC program and created the TANF block grant.

Categorical grants are sums of money provided by the federal government to the states for specified services for a "category" of individuals who are eligible. The grant monies must be spent according to federal rules and regulations, and the state has much less leeway in determining eligibility for a categorical program than it would under a block grant.

The **debt** is the accumulation of deficits over several years, including both principal and interest.

The **deficit** refers to a shortfall between expenditures and revenues in any given year.

Department of Health and Human Services (HHS) is the federal agency that is responsible for the implementation of welfare policy.

Dependency is the term used to describe those poor people who cannot stay out of poverty without government assistance. In general, the "unworthy" poor are considered to be dependent on welfare. Current attempts to reform welfare focus on reducing dependency by making welfare less attractive than work, in the hope that people in poverty can become self-sufficient rather than reliant on government programs. Liberals tend not to like the term dependency since it applies only to those people on welfare and implies that they do not deserve government assistance. (People on social security are not generally considered to be "dependent" on government assistance.)

Deserving poor are those who fall into poverty through no fault of their own. Examples include the elderly and the disabled. In general, these are the people who most Americans agree should be given government assistance. Programs aimed at the "deserving poor" (also called the "worthy poor")—social security and unemployment compensation, for example—generally are more popular than those aimed at the "undeserving" poor.

Devolution is the process of turning federal programs such as welfare back to the states to administer and operate.

Economic Opportunity Act of 1964 was the centerpiece of Lyndon Johnson's War on Poverty (also known as the Great Society). It set up the Office of Economic Opportunity at the federal level to administer new poverty programs.

Entitlements are federal programs to which certain individuals are "entitled" by law. Usually, categorical grants are provided for entitlement programs. Open-ended entitlements differ from block grants in that the federal government is required to spend money for every individual that qualifies for the program. A closed-end entitlement puts a cap on the amount that may be spent.

The **Family Assistance Plan (FAP)** was a welfare plan proposed by President Nixon. It would have eliminated AFDC entirely and replaced it with a guaranteed minimum income.

Family cap is a provision in state welfare laws that cuts benefits to families in which more children are born while the family is on welfare.

The **Family Support Act of 1988** was the last major revision of welfare before the PRWORA. The FSA increased work requirements for welfare recipients in return for beefing up supportive services such as job training, child care, and transportation costs.

Food stamps are vouchers to be used only for food purchases. Eligibility for food stamps is based on income. Food stamp fraud—selling food stamps for money to purchase drugs, for example—is often cited as a major problem in welfare. Food stamps are in-kind assistance: Rather than giving families extra cash, the government gives them vouchers to ensure the money will be spent properly.

Formula grants are federal grants given to the states on the basis of a "formula," usually determined by the population and income of the state and other characteristics deemed important for the program.

General assistance is a program run in 23 states to provide income assistance to people who "fall through the cracks" of federal poverty programs.

The **Great Society** is the name given to the series of poverty programs passed during the presidential administration of Lyndon Baines Johnson in the 1960s. The name implies that the programs were to create a society in which there was no poverty. The term Great Society is often used interchangeably with the War on Poverty.

Hoovervilles were encampments of homeless and destitute people set up on the outskirts of cities during the depression. The term reflects the antipathy the public felt toward President Hoover, who seemed unmoved by the widespread poverty of the depression.

Incrementalism refers to the tendency in American politics to change policies a little at a time (incrementally). It is often argued that the United States does not have major policy changes because of the structure of the policy process.

Individual (as the cause of poverty) is the belief which focuses on the individual rather than society or the economic structure as the cause of poverty. Those who believe in individualism feel that government programs encourage dependency. Current welfare reform attributes welfare dependence to a lack of individual initiative.

Indoor relief refers to poverty assistance given to individuals in institutions, such as poorhouses or hospitals, as opposed to outdoor relief, which was usually cash assistance. The term was used in the 1800s, when it was felt that the best way to handle poverty was to institutionalize the poor rather than give them cash assistance.

Keynesian economic theory was the basis for much of the New Deal and economic policies afterward. It advocates increasing government spending in order to increase income and employment.

Matching grants are often required for categorical or block grants. The federal government gives the state a percentage of the total cost of a particular program, and the state and/or local governments are required to provide the rest. For example, a program may have a 50–50 state match, in which the federal government puts in 50 percent of the required funding and the state provides the remaining 50 percent.

Medicaid is medical insurance for the poor. It is a federal program which uses federal and state funds. Medicaid benefits have in the past been tied to receipt of welfare, making it difficult for families to leave AFDC for low-paying jobs since they would no longer be eligible for medical assistance.

Mothers' pensions were the state laws which provided for monetary assistance to widows with children. They were one of the precursors to the AFDC program.

The **New Deal** refers to a series of programs undertaken by President Franklin Roosevelt to alleviate the impact of the Great Depression. The programs were passed by Congress and included such things as Aid to Dependent Children (ADC), unemployment insurance, work programs, and assistance to the elderly. The centerpiece of the New Deal was the Social Security Act of 1935. The New Deal provided social insurance for broad categories of Americans.

Outdoor relief is relief (or assistance) provided outside of governmental institutions. It generally refers to cash assistance.

Pauperism is a term that was used to describe the unworthy poor. A pauper was a person who became poor because of his or her own laziness, immorality, or sinfulness.

The **Personal Responsibility and Work Opportunity Reconciliation Act** (PRWORA) is the welfare reform legislation passed under the Republican Contract with America and signed into law by President Clinton on August 22, 1996. The legislation ends the entitlement status of welfare, eliminates the AFDC program (replacing it with TANF block grants to the states), requires welfare clients to engage in work within two years of receipt of welfare, cuts spending on the food stamp program, and eliminates benefits to legal aliens.

Poorhouses were institutions which housed the poor as a means of assistance. Conditions in the poorhouses were deplorable. They were used to deter people from asking for assistance, and they were supposed to rehabilitate people's behavior.

Redistributive programs use tax money from one group to pay benefits for another. For example, taxes on the middle class and wealthy may be used to pay for programs for the poor. Young working people may pay taxes which are used to pay for retirement programs for the elderly. The money is redistributed from one group to another.

Revenue sharing began during the Nixon administration, when the federal government redistributed money to the states with no strings attached. It was one of the first attempts at devolution.

Safety net is a way to describe government social programs that are supposed to catch individuals when they fall onto hard times. The safety net is expected to be available to the deserving poor but is not supposed to be so extensive that it causes dependence on government programs.

Scientific charity was a movement during the latter part of the nineteenth century when various societies decided to help the poor by home visits, consultations, and encouragement of middle-class values. The idea was to give aid through friendship rather than cash assistance.

Settlement houses were part of the progressive movement of the early 1900s. Settlement houses were placed in poor urban neighborhoods where middle-class reformers sought to teach poor immigrants practical skills and assimilate them into American culture.

Social Darwinism took the concept of "survival of the fittest" to an extreme. According to this theory, the poor should be left to fend for themselves, letting the best rise to the top and survive, while the worst elements would die out.

Social insurance refers to programs for individuals who are temporarily or permanently unable to work because of disability or old age, for example. Social insurance requires that individuals contribute a portion of their taxes specifically for the program, giving the impression that the program is not redistributive.

Social Security Act of 1935 (SSA) was the centerpiece of the New Deal. It created Old Age Assistance, now referred to as "social security," as well as what we now know as welfare.

Stigma implies shame, disgrace, or dishonor. Welfare programs "have a stigma attached" to them because societal values prefer work over welfare.

Structural interpretations of poverty place the root cause of poverty on the economic system rather than on the individual. According to such theories, some number of people will always end up in poverty as a result of capitalism, and it is the government's (as well as society's) responsibility to assist them.

Supplemental Security Income (SSI) is a federal program that provides income assistance to the disabled, including children as well as adults. The program has come under attack in recent years because eligibility requirements have enabled alcoholics and drug abusers as well as children with learning deficit disorders to receive benefits. Many people believe that SSI is subject to fraud because of these populations.

Temporary Assistance for Needy Families is the block grant that replaces the AFDC program. TANF, as created in the Personal Responsibility and Work Opportunity

Reconciliation Act (PRWORA), ends the entitlement status of welfare, creates a lifetime limit of five years for receipt of benefits, and requires recipients to work within two years.

Undeserving poor are the "able-bodied" poor. Because of the emphasis on individualism in the United States, those people who are capable of work are not considered to be "deserving" of government assistance. Those who believe poverty is a structural problem find the distinction between deserving and undeserving poor to be problematic since they feel it is the economic structure, not individual failings, that causes poverty.

Unemployment compensation is a social insurance program to which individuals contribute through payroll taxes. In the event that a person loses a job, unemployment compensation provides them money while they look for another.

Unworthy poor is a synonym for undeserving poor.

Waivers are exemptions from the rules of government programs. Under President Ronald Reagan, states began to receive waivers from the rules of AFDC to give them more leeway to create innovative welfare reform. Waivers are granted based on a state's application to the federal government, explaining why the rules of the categorical grant should be waived. With the new TANF block grant, the need for waivers has been eliminated.

The **War on Poverty** is the series of programs proposed by President Lyndon Johnson to alleviate the residual poverty that remained under an expanding economy. Much of the legislation was also directed at assisting African Americans. War on Poverty programs focused on increasing opportunities for individuals to bring themselves out of poverty, in contrast to the New Deal programs which tended to focus on social insurance. War on Poverty programs have been criticized in recent decades for causing dependence on government assistance.

Welfare refers to programs under which the federal government gives cash grants to individuals who fall below a certain income. In the past, the word has been used interchangeably with Aid to Families with Dependent Children (AFDC), which has been replaced by a block grant to the states. Welfare can also be used synonymously with well-being and could thus be used to describe any number of programs that provide for the well-being of citizens, from social security to student loans. In current usage, however, it is limited to programs specifically for the poor.

Worthy poor is a synonym for deserving poor.

Notes

Chapter 1

1. Linda Gordon, *Pitied but Not Entitled: Single Mothers and the History of Welfare, 1890–1935* (New York: Free Press, 1994), p. 1.

2. Thomas J. Corbett, "Welfare Reform in Wisconsin: The Rhetoric and the Reality," in Donald F. Norris and Lyke Thompson, eds., *The Politics of Welfare Reform* (London: Sage Publications 1995), pp. 19–20.

3. Susan Tolchin, *The Angry American: How Voter Rage Is Changing the Nation* (Boulder: Westview Press, 1996), p. 133.

4. U.S. Congress, House Committee on Ways and Means, *Overview of Entitlement Programs: 1994 Greenbook,* 103rd Congress, 2nd Session, 1994, p. 440.

5. David E. Rosenbaum, "The Welfare Enigma," *New York Times,* February 10, 1995, p. A16.

6. Douglas Besharov, "Welfare As We Know It," *Slate,* on-line magazine, July 12, 1996. Available on-line: www.slate.com/Gist/96-07-12/Gist.asp.

7. Jill Quadagno, *The Color of Welfare: How Racism Undermined the War on Poverty* (New York, Oxford: Oxford University Press, 1994), p. 14.

8. Blanche D. Coll, *Safety Net: Welfare and Social Security, 1929–1979* (New Brunswick, NJ: Rutgers University Press, 1995), p. 2; and Samuel Mencher, *Poor Law to Poverty Program* (Pittsburgh: University of Pittsburgh Press, 1967), p. 37.

9. Michael B. Katz, *In the Shadow of the Poorhouse: A Social History of Welfare in America* (New York: Basic Books, 1986), p. xiii.

10. Randy Albelda, Nancy Folbre, and The Center for Popular Economics, *The War on the Poor: A Defense Manual* (New York: New Press, 1994), p. 44.

11. Coll, *Safety Net,* pp. 104–105.

12. Besharov, "Welfare As We Know It."

13. Coll, *Safety Net,* p. 43.

14. Frances Fox Piven and Richard A. Cloward, *Regulating the Poor: The Functions of Public Welfare* (New York: Random House, Vintage Books edition, 1972), p. 165.

15. Quoted in Melinda Henneberger, "Welfare Bashing Finds Its Mark," *New York Times,* March 5, 1995, p. E5.

Chapter 2

1. Aid to Families with Dependent Children is a New Deal program; has been eliminated and replaced with the Temporary Assistance for Needy Families (TANF) block grant.

2. Edward Berkowitz, *America's Welfare State: From Roosevelt to Reagan* (Baltimore: Johns Hopkins University Press, 1991), p. 8.

3. See Frances Fox Piven and Richard Cloward, *Regulating the Poor: The Functions of Public Welfare* (New York: Random House, Vintage Books edition, 1972), pp. 3–41.

4. See Stuart Butler and Anna Kondratas, *Out of the Poverty Trap: A Conservative Strategy for Welfare Reform* (New York: Free Press, 1987), p. 30; Walter I. Trattner, *From Poor Law to Welfare State: A History of Social Welfare in America* (New York: Free Press, 1984), p. 5.

5. Trattner, *From Poor Law to Welfare State*, p. 11.

6. Piven and Cloward, *Regulating the Poor*, p. 130.

7. Butler and Kondratas, *Out of the Poverty Trap*, p. 30.

8. Trattner, *From Poor Law to Welfare State*, p. 49.

9. Ibid., pp. 18–19.

10. Samuel Mencher, *Poor Law to Poverty Program: Economic Security Policy in Britain and the United States* (Pittsburgh: University of Pittsburgh Press, 1967), p. 40.

11. Trattner, *From Poor Law to Welfare State*, p. 24.

12. Marvin Olaskey, *The Tragedy of American Compassion* (Washington, DC: Regnery Gateway, 1992).

13. Trattner, *From Poor Law to Welfare State*, pp. 38, 53.

14. Ibid., pp. 53–54.

15. Ralph Segalman, "The Protestant Ethic and Social Welfare," *Journal of Social Issues* 24 (1968): 126.

16. Michael B. Katz, *In the Shadow of the Poorhouse: A Social History of Welfare in America* (New York: Basic Books, Inc., 1986), p. 14.

17. Lyke Thompson and Donald F. Norris, "Introduction: The Politics of Welfare Reform," in Donald F. Norris and Lyke Thompson, eds., *The Politics of Welfare Reform* (London: Sage Publications, 1995), p. 4.

18. See Jill Quadagno, *The Color of Welfare: How Racism Undermined the War on Poverty* (New York, Oxford: Oxford University Press, 1994).

19. Katz, *In the Shadow of the Poorhouse*, p. 24.

20. Ibid., p. 35.

21. Ibid., p. 19.

22. Edward Berkowitz and Kim McQuaid, *Creating the Welfare State: The Political Economy of Twentieth Century Reform* (New York, Westport, CT, and London: Praeger, 1988), p. 36.

23. Josephine Shaw Lowell, *Public Relief and Private Charity* (New York and London: G. P. Putnam's Sons, Knickerbocker Press, 1884; reprint, New York: Arno Press and *New York Times*, 1971), p. 96.

24. Trattner, *From Poor Law to Welfare State*, p. 67.

25. Ibid., p. 55.

26. Ibid., p. 70.

27. In fact, according to Katz, in *In the Shadow of the Poorhouse*, the Catholic Church took a different approach to dealing with poverty than did the American reformers. Catholic charity "was less judgmental, more ready to help and less quick to condemn" and at the same time, "sought to alleviate the suffering of the poor rather than prevent it. . . . Efforts made by the Catholic Church to help the sick and the needy can only be described as heroic. An immigrant, working-class institution, the Catholic Church lacked the resources available to the Protestant community. Even so, it built major institutions and devoted a great share of its resources to the poor" (pp. 61–62).

28. James T. Patterson, *America's Struggle Against Poverty, 1900–1980* (Cambridge and London: Harvard University Press, 1981), p. 23.

29. See Patterson, *America's Struggle Against Poverty;* Linda Gordon, *Pitied but Not Entitled: Single Mothers and the History of Welfare, 1890–1935* (New York: Free Press, 1994).

30. See Gwendolyn Mink, *The Wages of Motherhood: Inequality in the Welfare State, 1917–1942* (Ithaca: Cornell University Press, 1995), p. 13.

31. Gordon, *Pitied but Not Entitled*, p. 44.

32. Mink, *The Wages of Motherhood*, pp. 13–14.

33. Patterson, *America's Struggle Against Poverty*, p. 24.

34. Ibid., p. 25.

35. This movement, led by Charles Brace, had both positive and negative results. On the positive side, many children were taken out of slum conditions and sent to live with farming families where they learned valuable skills and were given opportunities far beyond what they would have had in the city. On the other hand, sometimes the farm families treated the city children as little more than indentured servants, overworking or otherwise abusing them. And many immigrant families did not appreciate having their children taken from them to be brought up in another culture and religion.

36. Gordon, *Pitied but Not Entitled*, p. 96.

37. See Patterson, *America's Struggle Against Poverty;* and Gordon, *Pitied but Not Entitled*.

38. "Desertion" was a big problem early in this century for the simple reason that poor people couldn't afford to get divorces. A poor woman whose husband had left her had a hard time getting assistance from social workers because they feared that aid to deserted wives would encourage husbands to leave. (See Gordon, *Pitied but Not Entitled*, p. 26.) Thus, the debate over mothers' pensions is similar to the debate over welfare today: Both deal with poverty assistance as a cause of family breakdown.

39. Berkowitz, *America's Welfare State*, p. 96.

40. Mink, *The Wages of Motherhood*, p. 29.

41. Gordon, *Pitied but Not Entitled*, p. 38.

42. Trattner, *From Poor Law to Welfare State*, p. 247.

43. Katz, *In the Shadow of the Poorhouse*, p. 207.

44. Quoted in Samuel Mencher, *Poor Law to Poverty Program*, p. 383.

45. Trattner, *From Poor Law to Poverty Program*, p. 260.

46. William E. Leuchtenburg, *Franklin Delano Roosevelt and the New Deal, 1932–1940* (New York: Harper and Row, 1963).

47. The phrase "New Deal" was not intended by Roosevelt to be the name of his domestic program. He used the words in his acceptance speech at the Democratic nominating convention, and a cartoonist picked them out the next day, christening Roosevelt's anti-depression policies with the name that stuck. See Leuchtenburg, *Roosevelt and the New Deal,* p. 8.

48. Roosevelt's ability to push so many programs through Congress during his first one hundred days in office has created a standard by which subsequent presidents have been judged. It has become common now for there to be an evaluation of a president's capabilities on or around his hundredth day in office, during his first term.

49. Blanche D. Coll, *Safety Net: Welfare and Social Security, 1929–1979* (New Brunswick, NJ: Rutgers University Press, 1995), p. 50.

50. Patterson, *America's Struggle Against Poverty,* pp. 70–71.

51. Coll, *Safety Net,* p. 103.

52. Ibid., pp. 104–105.

53. Patterson, *America's Struggle Against Poverty,* p. 60.

54. Berkowitz, *America's Welfare State,* p. 91.

55. Quoted in Patterson, *America's Struggle Against Poverty,* p. 59.

56. Trattner, *From Poor Law to Welfare State,* p. 264.

57. "European countries have devoted a much larger share of their GNP, of their public funds, to bettering the living conditions of the working classes and the less privileged generally." Seymour Martin Lipset, *American Exceptionalism: A Double-Edged Sword* (New York, London: W. W. Norton, 1996), p. 22.

58. Patterson, *America's Struggle Against Poverty,* pp. 45–46.

59. Mink, *The Wages of Motherhood,* pp. 135–138.

60. Coll, *Safety Net,* p. 176.

61. Ibid., p. 192.

62. Ibid., p. 186.

63. President Kennedy read Michael Harrington's book and then created a task force to study the issue of poverty in the United States. After Kennedy's assassination in 1963, President Johnson inherited the results of the task force, which he used as the impetus for his War on Poverty, pushing Harrington's book onto the bestseller list. See James T. Patterson, *America's Struggle Against Poverty,* p. 99.

64. Wilbur J. Cohen, Assistant Secretary of HEW, *Notes from the Seminar on Poverty in Plenty* (Washington, DC: Georgetown University Institute of Social Ethics, January 23, 1964), p. 102.

65. Patterson, *America's Struggle Against Poverty,* p. 137.

66. By 1948, "certain words,—'socialist,' 'socialized,' even 'welfare' as in 'welfare state'—acquired a Communist aura and were frequently used as proofs of disloyalty. In this emotion-laden context social reform lost much of its former prestige." (Coll, *Safety Net,* p. 152.)

67. Quadagno, *The Color of Welfare,* p. 33.

68. Ibid., pp. 35–41.

69. Butler and Kondratas, *Out of the Poverty Trap.*

70. Ibid., p. 8.

71. The ADC grant initially went only to the children of a family. In 1950, program requirements were changed so that assistance went to the mother as well as to her children, thus the name change to include "families." In 1961, AFDC was expanded to include fathers, at state option.

72. Anne Marie Cammisa, *Governments as Interest Groups: Intergovernmental Lobbying and the Federal System* (Westport, CT: Praeger Press, 1995), p. 91.

73. Patterson, *America's Struggle Against Poverty,* p. 153.

74. Ibid., p. 55.

75. Berkowitz, *America's Welfare State,* p. 111.

76. FAP actually was an outgrowth of a Johnson presidential commission, the President's Commission on Income Maintenance, which issued a report called *From Poverty Amid Plenty: The American Paradox.* The report recommended creating a negative income tax. Lyndon Johnson and members of his administration opposed the recommendations, preferring to continue with programs to "rehabilitate" the poor. Nixon, who inherited the results of the report on taking office, did not have the same commitment to the rehabilitation approach and embraced the recommendations of the commission. Berkowitz, *America's Welfare State,* p. 123.

77. Patterson, *America's Struggle Against Poverty,* p. 193.

78. Quadagno, *The Color of Welfare,* pp. 122–123.

79. Berkowitz, *America's Welfare State,* p. 123.

80. Ibid., pp. 127–130.

81. See Quadagno, *The Color of Welfare.*

82. Patterson, *America's Struggle Against Poverty,* pp. 194–195.

83. Thompson and Norris, "Introduction: The Politics of Welfare Reform."

84. David Stoesz, *Small Change: Domestic Policy Under the Clinton Presidency* (White Plains, NY: Longman, 1996), p. 13.

85. Gordon, *Pitied but Not Entitled,* p. 288.

86. Quadagno, *The Color of Welfare,* p. 162.

87. Stoesz, *Small Change,* p. 63.

88. Cammisa, *Governments as Interest Groups,* p. 89.

Chapter 3

1. See Michael T. Hayes, *Incrementalism and Public Policy* (New York: Longman, 1992).

2. Stoesz, *Small Change: Domestic Policy Under the Clinton Presidency* (White Plains, NY: Longman), p. 72.

3. Jeffrey L. Katz and David S. Cloud, "Welfare Overhaul Leaves Dole with Campaign Dilemma," *Congressional Quarterly Weekly Report,* April 20, 1996, p. 1025.

4. Robert Pear, "Dole Postpones Further Debate on Welfare Bill," *New York Times,* August 9, 1995, p. A1.

5. "Social Policy. Issue: Welfare," *Congressional Quarterly Weekly Report Special Report,* September 2, 1995, p. 2643. See also Barbara Vobejda, "Dole Faces GOP Rifts on Welfare," *Washington Post,* September 6, 1995, p. A15.

6. "Social Policy. Issue: Welfare," *Congressional Quarterly Weekly Report Special Report,* January 6, 1996, pp. 37–38.

7. Robin Toner, "A Six-Decade-Old Policy Is Turned Aside on a Vote of 87 to 12," *New York Times,* September 19, 1995, p. B1.

8. Robin Toner, "Senate Approves Welfare Plan That Would End Aid Guarantee," *New York Times,* September 20, 1995, p. A1.

9. "Social Policy. Issue: Welfare," *Congressional Quarterly Special Report,* January 6, 1996, p. 37.

10. "As Expected, Clinton Vetoes Welfare Overhaul Bill," *Congressional Quarterly Weekly Report,* January 13, 1996, p. 95.

11. Bob Woodward, *The Choice* (New York: Simon and Schuster, 1996).

12. Jeffrey L. Katz, "GOP Prepares to Act on Governors' Plan," *Congressional Quarterly Weekly Report,* February 17, 1996, p. 394.

13. Jeffrey L. Katz, "Voter Call for Revamped Welfare Poses Problem for Democrats," *Congressional Quarterly Weekly Report,* April 20, 1996, p. 1029.

14. Katz and Cloud, "Welfare Overhaul," p. 1023.

15. Woodward, *The Choice,* p. 431.

16. Jeffrey L. Katz, "Ignoring Veto Threat, GOP Links Welfare, Medicaid," *Congressional Quarterly Weekly Report,* May 25, 1996, p. 1467.

17. Ibid., p. 1467.

18. Ibid.

19. Jeffrey L. Katz, "GOP's New Welfare Strategy Has Democrats Reassessing," *Congressional Quarterly Weekly Report,* July 13, 1996, p. 1969.

20. Judith Havemann, "GOP Calls President's 'Bluff' on Welfare," *Washington Post,* July 12, 1996, p. A20.

21. Ibid.

22. Jeffrey L. Katz, "Conferees May Determine Fate of Overhaul Bill," *Congressional Quarterly Weekly Report,* July 20, 1996, p. 2048.

23. Robert Pear, "President Says Cuts Are Too Deep in Republican Welfare Plan," *New York Times,* July 18, 1996, p. A21.

24. Robert Pear, "Budget Agency Says Welfare Bill Would Cut Rolls by Millions," *New York Times,* July 16, 1996, p. A12.

25. Katz, "Conferees May Determine Fate," p. 2048.

26. Robert Pear, "House Approves Shift on Welfare," *New York Times,* July 19, 1996, p. A1.

27. Robert Pear, "Gore Says He Expects an Accord on Welfare," *New York Times,* July 22, 1996, p. A13.

28. "Clinton Will Sign Bill, Dole Asserts," *New York Times,* July 23, 1996, p. A11.

29. Robert Pear, "Senate Approves Sweeping Change in Welfare Policy," *New York Times,* July 24, 1996, p. A1.

30. Ibid.

31. Jeffrey L. Katz, "Welfare Showdown Looms as GOP Readies Plan," *Congressional Quarterly Weekly Report,* July 27, 1996, p. 2116.

32. Ibid.

33. Todd S. Purdum, "Clinton Recalls His Promise, Weighs History, and Decides," *New York Times,* August 1, 1996, p. A1.

34. Evan Thomas, *Back from the Dead* (New York: Atlantic Monthly Press, 1997), p. 136.

35. Thomas, *Back from the Dead,* p. 135.

36. Purdum, "Clinton Recalls His Promise," p. A1.

37. Robert Pear, "Clinton to Sign Welfare Bill That Ends U.S. Aid Guarantee and Gives States Broad Power," *New York Times,* August 1, 1996, p. A22.

38. Lawrence L. Knutson, "Clinton Signs Welfare Bill," *Washington Post,* August 22, 1996. Available on-line: www.washingtonpost.com/wp-srv/digest/nat2.htm.

Chapter 4

1. Joel F. Handler, *The Poverty of Welfare Reform* (New Haven and London: Yale University Press, 1995), p. 33.

2. U.S. Congress, House Committee on Ways and Means, *Overview of Entitlement Programs: 1994 Greenbook* (103rd Congress, 2nd Session, 1994), Appendix H, Data on Poverty.

3. Handler, *The Poverty of Welfare Reform,* p. 34.

4. Randy Albelda, Nancy Folbre, and The Center for Popular Economics, *The War on the Poor: A Defense Manual* (New York: New Press, 1994), p. 13. See also Patricia Ruggles, *Drawing the Line: Alternative Poverty Measures and Their Implications for Policy* (Washington, DC: Urban Institute Press, 1990); Trudi Renwick and Barbara Bergmann, "A Budget-Based Definition of Poverty, With an Application to Single-Parent Families," *Journal of Human Resources* 28, no. 1 (Winter 1993):1–24.

5. U.S. Congress, *1994 Greenbook.*

6. Louis Uchitelle, "Welfare Recipients Taking Jobs Often Held by the Working Poor," *New York Times,* April 1, 1997, p. A16.

7. Blanche D. Coll, *Safety Net: Welfare and Social Security, 1929–1979* (New Brunswick, NJ: Rutgers University Press, 1995), p. 33; and James T. Patterson, *America's Struggle Against Poverty, 1900–1980* (Cambridge and London: Harvard University Press, 1981), p. 85.

8. Patterson, *America's Struggle Against Poverty,* p. 151.

9. James J. Gosling, *Budgetary Politics in American Governments* (New York and London: Longman, 1992), p. 45.

10. Spencer Rich, "Reagan Welfare Proposal Criticized by Agencies," *Washington Post,* February 10, 1987, p. A8.

11. Charles Murray, *Losing Ground: American Social Policy, 1950–1980* (New York: Basic Books, 1984).

12. Michael B. Katz, *In the Shadow of the Poorhouse: A Social History of Welfare in America* (New York: Basic Books, 1986), p. 18.

13. Robert Pear, "A Welfare Revolution Hits Home, But Quietly," *New York Times,* August 13, 1995, p. A1.

14. Peter Kilborn and Sam Howe Verhovek, "Welfare Shift Reflects New Democrat," *New York Times,* August 2, 1996.

15. Bill Clinton and Al Gore, *Putting People First: How We Can All Change America* (New York: Times Books, 1992), pp. 164–168.

16. Peter G. Gosselin, "Welfare Analyst Exits D.C. Fray," *Boston Globe,* August 5, 1995, pp. 1, 20–21.

17. Ibid.

18. Kilborn and Verhovek, "Welfare Shift Reflects New Democrat."

19. Ibid.

20. Douglas Besharov, "Welfare As We Know It," *Slate,* July 12, 1996. Available on-line: www.slate.com/Gist/96-07-12/Gist.asp.

21. Jeffrey Katz, "Putting Recipients to Work Will Be the Toughest Job," *Congressional Quarterly Weekly Report,* July 18, 1995, p. 2001.

22. Handler, *The Poverty of Welfare Reform,* p. 117.

23. Ibid., p. 117.

24. Jon Nordheimer, "Welfare-to-Work Plans Show Success Is Difficult to Achieve," *New York Times,* September 1, 1996, pp. 1, 18.

25. Judith Gueron, *Reforming Welfare with Work,* Occasional Paper 2 (New York: Ford Foundation Project on Social Welfare and the American Future, 1987).

26. Stuart Butler and Anna Kondratas, *Out of the Poverty Trap: A Conservative Strategy for Welfare Reform* (New York: Free Press, 1987), p. 138.

27. Indeed, First Lady Hillary Clinton's book, *It Takes a Village* (New York: Simon and Schuster, 1996), much-maligned at the 1996 Republican national convention, follows on the footsteps of the longing for a more traditional family. In it, she reminisces about growing up "in a family that looked like it was straight out of the 1950s television sitcom *Father Knows Best*" (p. 20).

28. Butler and Kondratas, *Out of the Poverty Trap,* p. 243.

29. Kilborn and Verhovek, "Welfare Shift Reflects New Democrat."

30. Daniel Patrick Moynihan, *The Negro Family: The Case for National Action* (Washington, DC: U.S. Government Printing Office, 1965).

31. Edward Berkowitz, *America's Welfare State: From Roosevelt to Reagan* (Baltimore: Johns Hopkins University Press, 1991), pp. 125–126; see also E. J. Dionne, *Why Americans Hate Politics* (New York: Touchstone, 1991), p. 55. Dionne explains that the label "neoconservative" was applied to a group of moderate intellectuals, including Moynihan, who called themselves liberals. Michael Harrington, a democratic socialist, derisively called them neoconservatives, and the name stuck.

32. William Julius Wilson, *The Truly Disadvantaged: The Inner City, the Underclass, and Public Policy* (Chicago: University of Chicago Press, 1987).

33. Teresa L. Amott, "Black Women and AFDC: Making Entitlement Out of Necessity," Chapter 12 in Linda Gordon, ed., *Women, the State, and Welfare* (Madison: University of Wisconsin Press, 1990), pp. 282–287.

34. Barbara Vobejda and Helen Dewar, "Bill to Overhaul Welfare Clears Senate, 74–24," *Washington Post*, July 24, 1996, p. A6.

35. Barbara Vobejda, "House Passes Major Overhaul of Nation's Welfare Programs," *Washington Post*, July 19, 1996, p. A1.

36. Guy Gugliotta and Ruth Marcus, "Election-Year Politics Help Democrats Deal with Differences on Welfare," *Washington Post*, August 2, 1996, p. A8.

37. Patterson, *America's Struggle Against Poverty*, p. 59.

38. Trattner, *From Poor Law to Welfare State*, p. 264.

39. Kilborn and Verhovek, "Welfare Shift Reflects New Democrat."

40. Judith Havemann, "Scholars Question Whether Welfare Shift Is Reform," *Washington Post*, April 20, 1995.

41. Jeffrey Katz, "Members Pushing to Retain Welfare System Control," *Congressional Quarterly Weekly Reports*, January 28, 1995, p. 281.

42. Lawrence L. Knutson, "Clinton Signs Welfare Bill," *Washington Post*, August 22, 1996, p. A1.

43. Isabel Sawhill and Sheila Zedlewski, "A Million More Poor Children," *Washington Post*, July 26, 1996, p. A27.

44. Lawrence Mead and Gary Burtless are quoted in Jeffrey Katz, "Putting Recipients to Work Will Be the Toughest Job," *Congressional Quarterly Weekly Report*, July 18, 1995, p. 2005.

45. William J. Bennett, "A Welfare Test," *Washington Post*, August 18, 1996, p. C7.

Chapter 5

1. Alison Mitchell, "Two Clinton Aides Resign to Protest New Welfare Law," *New York Times*, September 12, 1996, p. A1.

2. Peter Kilborn, "With Welfare Overhaul Now Law, States Grapple with the Consequences," *New York Times*, August 23, 1996, p. A22.

3. Robert Pear, "Welfare Changes, While Big, Will Be Taking Shape Slowly," *New York Times*, August 6, 1996, p. A9.

4. Robert Pear, "Most States Find Goals on Welfare Within Easy Reach," *New York Times*, September 3, 1996, p. B6.

5. Judith Havemann and Barbara Vobejda, "Drop in Welfare Leads to Fight for the Credit," *Washington Post*, May 13, 1996, p. A1.

6. Quoted in Robert Pear, "Action by States Hold Keys to Welfare Law's Future," *New York Times*, October 1, 1996, p. A22.

7. Robert Pear, "Clinton Cites Welfare Gains and Defends Overhaul Plans," *New York Times*, December 8, 1996, p. A35.

8. Pear, "Most States Find Goals on Welfare Within Easy Reach," p. A1.

9. Barbara Vobejda, "HHS Official Resigns in Protest of Decision to Sign Welfare Bill," *Washington Post*, August 18, 1996.

10. Mitchell, "Two Clinton Aides Resign," p. A1.

11. Peter Gosselin, "Welfare Analyst Leaves D.C. Fray," *Boston Globe*, August 5, 1995, pp. 1, 20–21.

12. Robert Pear, "State Welfare Chiefs Ask for More U.S. Guidance," *New York Times*, September 10, 1996.

13. Ibid.

14. Robert Pear, "So Far States Aren't Rewriting the Book on Welfare," *New York Times*, October 15, 1996, p. A21.

15. Robert Pear, "A Computer Gap Is Likely to Slow Welfare Changes," *New York Times*, September 1, 1996, p. A1.

16. Robert Pear, "Clinton Considers Move to Soften Cuts in Welfare," *New York Times*, November 27, 1996, p. A1.

17. Ibid.

18. Robert Pear, "Administration Welfare Plea Is Scorned," *New York Times*, February 14, 1997.

19. William J. Bennett, "A Welfare Test," *Washington Post*, August 18, 1996, p. C7.

References

Albelda, Randy, Nancy Folbre, and The Center for Popular Economics. *The War on the Poor: A Defense Manual.* New York: New Press, 1994.

Amott, Teresa L. "Black Women and AFDC: Making Entitlement out of Necessity." Chapter 12 in Linda Gordon, ed., *Women, the State, and Welfare.* Madison: University of Wisconsin Press, 1990.

Anderson, James E. *Public Policymaking: An Introduction.* 2nd ed. Boston and Toronto: Houghton-Mifflin, 1994.

"As Expected, Clinton Vetoes Welfare Overhaul Bill," *Congressional Quarterly Weekly Report,* January 13, 1996, p. 95.

Bennett, William J. "A Welfare Test," *Washington Post,* August 18, 1996.

Berkowitz, Edward. *America's Welfare State: From Roosevelt to Reagan.* Baltimore: Johns Hopkins University Press, 1991.

Berkowitz, Edward, and Kim McQuaid. *Creating the Welfare State: The Political Economy of Twentieth-Century Reform.* New York, Westport, CT, London: Praeger, 1988.

Besharov, Douglas. "Welfare As We Know It," *Slate,* July 12, 1996. Available on-line: www.slate.com/Gist/96-07-12/Gist.asp.

Bremner, Robert H. *The Discovery of Poverty in the United States.* New Brunswick, NJ, and London: Transaction Publishers, 1992.

Brown, Michael K., ed. *Remaking the Welfare State: Retrenchment and Social Policy in America and Europe.* Philadelphia: Temple University Press, 1988.

Butler, Stuart, and Anna Kondratas. *Out of the Poverty Trap: A Conservative Strategy for Welfare Reform.* New York: Free Press, 1987.

Cammisa, Anne Marie. *Governments As Interest Groups: Intergovernmental Lobbying and the Federal System.* Westport, CT: Praeger Press, 1995.

Chubb, John E., and Paul E. Peterson, eds. *The New Direction in American Politics.* Washington, DC: Brookings Institution, 1995.

Clinton, Hillary Rodham. *It Takes a Village and Other Lessons Children Teach Us.* New York: Simon and Schuster, 1996.

Clinton, William. "Clinton Welfare Text," *Washington Post,* August 22, 1996.

"Clinton Will Sign Bill, Dole Asserts," *New York Times,* July 23, 1996, p. A11.

Coll, Blanche D. *Safety Net: Social Welfare and Social Security, 1929–1979.* New Brunswick, NJ: Rutgers University Press, 1995.

Conlan, Timothy. *New Federalism: Intergovernmental Reform from Nixon to Reagan.* Washington, DC: Brookings Institution, 1988.

Corbett, Thomas J. "Welfare Reform in Wisconsin: The Rhetoric and the Reality." Chapter 2 in Donald F. Norris and Lyke Thompson, eds., *The Politics of Welfare Reform.* London: Sage Publications, 1995.

Davidson, Roger H., and Walter J. Oleszek. *Congress and Its Members.* Washington, DC: CQ Press, 1990.

Dobelstein, Andrew W. *Politics, Economics, and Welfare.* Englewood Cliffs, NJ: Prentice-Hall, 1986.

Galbraith, John Kenneth. *The Affluent Society,* 4th rev. ed. New York: New American Library, 1985.

Georgetown University, Institute of Social Ethics. Seminar. *Poverty in Plenty.* Gaston Hall, Georgetown University, Washington, DC, January 23, 1964.

Gillespie, Ed, and Bob Schellhas, eds. *Contract with America: The Bold Plan by Representative Newt Gingrich, Representative Dick Armey, and the House Republicans to Change the Nation.* New York: Random House, 1994.

Gleckman, Howard. "Rewriting the Social Contract." *Business Week,* November 20, 1995.

Goldberg v. Kelly, 397 U.S. 254 (1969).

Gordon, Linda. *Pitied but Not Entitled: Single Mothers and the History of Welfare, 1890–1935.* New York: Free Press, 1994.

_____, ed. *Women, the State, and Welfare.* Madison: University of Wisconsin Press, 1990.

Gosling, James J. *Budgetary Politics in American Governments.* New York and London: Longman, 1992.

Gosselin, Peter G. "Welfare Analyst Exits D.C. Fray." *Boston Globe,* August 5, 1995, pp. 1, 20–21.

Gottschalk, Barbara, and Peter Gottschalk. "The Reagan Retrenchment in Historical Context." Chapter 3 in Michael K. Brown, ed., *Remaking the Welfare State: Retrenchment and Social Policy in America and Europe.* Philadelphia: Temple University Press, 1988.

Greenberg, David, and H. Halsey. "Systematic Misreporting and Effects of Income Maintenance Experiments on Work Effort: Evidence from the Seattle-Denver Experiment." *Review of Economics and Statistics* 1: 380–407.

Greenberg, David, R. Moffit, and J. Friedman. "Underreporting and Experimental Effects on Work Effort: Evidence from the Gary Income Maintenance Experiment." *Review of Economics and Statistics* 63: 581–590.

Gross, Bertram M., ed. *A Great Society.* New York and London: Basic Books, 1968.

Gueron, Judith. *Work Initiatives for Welfare Recipients: Lessons from a Multistate Experiment.* New York: MDRC, 1986.

_____. *Reforming Welfare with Work,* Occasional Paper 2. New York: Ford Foundation Project on Social Welfare and the American Future, 1987.

_____. "Work and Welfare: Lessons on Employment Programs." *Journal of Economic Perspectives* (Winter 1990).

Handler, Joel F. *The Poverty of Welfare Reform.* New Haven and London: Yale University Press, 1995.

Handler, Joel F., and Yeheskel Hasenfeld. *The Moral Construction of Poverty: Welfare Reform in America*. Newbury Park, CA, London, New Delhi: Sage Publications, 1991.

Harrington, Michael. *The Other America: Poverty in the United States*, rev. ed. New York: Penguin Books, 1981.

Havemann, Judith. "GOP Calls President's 'Bluff' on Welfare." *Washington Post*, July 12, 1996, p. A20.

Havemann, Judith, and Barbara Vobejda. "Drop in Welfare Leads to Fight for the Credit." *Washington Post*, May 13, 1996, p. A1.

Hayes, Michael. *Incrementalism and Public Policy*. New York: Longman, 1992.

Henig, Jeffrey. *Public Policy and Federalism: Issues in State and Local Politics*. New York: St. Martin's Press, 1985.

Henneberger, Melinda. "Welfare Bashing Finds Its Mark." *New York Times*, March 5, 1995, Sec. E, p. 5.

Karger, Howard J. and David Stoesz. *American Social Welfare Policy: A Structural Approach*. New York and London: Longman, 1990.

Katz, Jeffrey L. "House Democrats Divide on Welfare." *Congressional Quarterly Weekly Report*, April 2, 1994, p. 801.

_____. "Putting Recipients to Work Will Be the Toughest Job." *Congressional Quarterly Weekly Report*, July 18, 1996, p. 2001.

_____. "GOP Prepares to Act on Governors' Plan." *Congressional Quarterly Weekly Report*, February 17, 1995, p. 394.

_____. "Voter Call for Revamped Welfare Poses Problem for Democrats." *Congressional Quarterly Weekly Report*, April 20, 1996, p. 1029.

_____. "Ignoring Veto Threat, GOP Links Welfare, Medicaid." *Congressional Quarterly Weekly Report*, May 25, 1996, p. 1467.

_____. "GOP's New Welfare Strategy Has Democrats Reassessing." *Congressional Quarterly Weekly Report*, July 13, 1996, p. 1969.

_____. "Conferees May Determine Fate of Overhaul Bill." *Congressional Quarterly Weekly Report*, July 20, 1996, p. 2048.

_____. "Welfare Showdown Looms as GOP Readies Plan." *Congressional Quarterly Weekly Report*, July 27, 1996, p. 2116.

_____. "Provisions: Welfare Overhaul Law." *Congressional Quarterly Weekly Report*, September 21, 1996, pp. 2696–2705.

Katz, Jeffrey L., and David S. Cloud. "Welfare Overhaul Leaves Dole with Campaign Dilemma." *Congressional Quarterly Weekly Report*, April 20, 1996, pp. 1023–1025.

Katz, Michael B. *In the Shadow of the Poorhouse: A Social History of Welfare in America*. New York: Basic Books, 1986.

_____. *Improving Poor People: The Welfare State, the "Underclass," and Urban Schools as History*. Princeton: Princeton University Press, 1995.

Kingdon, John. *Agendas, Alternatives, and Public Policies*, 2d ed. New York: HarperCollins College Publishers, 1995.

Leuchtenburg, William E. *Franklin Roosevelt and the New Deal 1932–1940*. New York: Harper and Row Publishers, 1963.

Levine, Herbert M., Neil B. Cohen, Joy E. Esberey, Thomas H. Farrell, Judith F. Gentry, Glen Jeansonne, and John J. Pitney, Jr. *What If the American Political System Were Different?* Armonk, NY, and London: M. E. Sharpe, 1992.

Lindbloom, Charles. *The Policy-Making Process*. Englewood Cliffs, NJ: Prentice-Hall, 1968.

Lipset, Seymour Martin. *American Exceptionalism: A Double-Edged Sword*. New York, London: W. W. Norton, 1996.

Lowell, Josephine Shaw. *Public Relief and Private Charity*. New York and London: G. P. Putnam's Sons and Knickerbocker Press, 1884; reprint, New York: Arno Press and New York Times, 1971.

Mackenzie, G. Calvin, and Saranna Thornton. *Bucking the Deficit: Economic Policymaking in America*. Boulder, CO: Westview Press, 1996.

Mead, Lawrence. *Beyond Entitlement: The Social Obligations of Citizenship*. New York: Free Press, 1985.

Mencher, Samuel. *Poor Law to Poverty Program: Economic Security in Britain and the United States*. Pittsburgh: University of Pittsburgh Press, 1967.

Mink, Gwendolyn. *The Wages of Motherhood: Inequality in the Welfare State, 1917–1942*. Ithaca: Cornell University Press, 1995.

Mitchell, Alison. "Two Clinton Aides Resign to Protest New Welfare Law." *New York Times*, September 6, 1996, p. A1.

Moynihan, Daniel Patrick. *The Negro Family: The Case for National Action*. Washington, DC: U.S. Government Printing Office, 1965.

Murray, Charles. *Losing Ground: American Social Policy, 1950–1980*. New York: Basic Books, 1994, 10th anniversary edition.

Nordheimer, Jon. "Welfare-to-Work Plans Show Success Is Difficult to Achieve." *New York Times*, September 1, 1996, pp. 1, 18.

Norris, Donald F., and Lyke Thompson, eds. *The Politics of Welfare Reform*. London: Sage Publications, 1995.

Olasky, Marvin. *The Tragedy of American Compassion*. Washington, DC: Regnery Publishing, 1992.

Patterson, James T. *America's Struggle Against Poverty, 1900–1980*. Cambridge and London: Harvard University Press, 1981.

Pear, Robert. "Dole Postpones Further Debate on Welfare Bill." *New York Times*, August 9, 1995, p. A1.

———. "A Welfare Revolution Hits Home, But Quietly." *New York Times*, August 13, 1995, pp. A1, A5.

———. "Budget Agency Says Welfare Bill Would Cut Rolls by Millions." *New York Times*, July 16, 1996, p. A12.

———. "President Says Cuts Are Too Deep in Republican Welfare Plan." *New York Times*, July 18, 1996, p. A21.

_____. "House Approves Shift on Welfare." *New York Times*, July 19, 1996, p. A1.

_____. "Gore Says He Expects an Accord on Welfare." *New York Times*, July 22, 1996, p. A13.

_____. "Senate Approves Sweeping Change in Welfare Policy." *New York Times*, July 24, 1996, p. A1.

_____. "Clinton to Sign Welfare Bill That Ends U.S. Aid Guarantee and Gives States Broad Power." *New York Times*, August 1, 1996, p. A22.

_____. "A Computer Gap Is Likely to Slow Welfare Changes." *New York Times*, September 1, 1996, p. A1.

_____. "Most States Find Goals on Welfare Within Easy Reach." *New York Times*, September 3, 1996, p. A1.

_____. "Action by States Holds Keys to Welfare Law's Future." *New York Times*, October 1, 1996, p. A22.

_____. "Clinton Cites Welfare Gains and Defends Overhaul Plans." *New York Times*, December 8, 1996, p. A35.

_____. "Administration Welfare Plea Is Scorned." *New York Times*, February 14, 1997.

Peters, B. Guy. *American Public Policy: Promise and Performance*, 2d ed. Chatham, NJ: Chatham House Publishers, 1986.

Pitney, John J., Jr. "What If There Were No Welfare State?" Chapter 9 in Herbert M. Levine, Neil B. Cohen, Joy E. Esberey, Thomas H. Farrell, Judith F. Gentry, Glen Jeansonne, and John J. Pitney, Jr. *What If the American Political System Were Different?* Armonk, NY, and London: M. E. Sharpe, 1992.

Piven, Frances Fox, and Richard A. Cloward. *Regulating the Poor: The Functions of Public Welfare*. New York: Random House, Vintage Books edition, 1972.

President's Commission on Income Maintenance. *From Poverty amid Plenty: The American Paradox*. Washington, DC: U.S. Government Printing Office, 1969.

Pressman, Jeffrey L., and Aaron Wildavsky. *Implementation: How Great Expectations in Washington Are Dashed in Oakland*. Berkeley: University of California Press, 1973.

Purdum, Todd S. "Clinton Recalls His Promise, Weighs History, and Decides." *New York Times*, August 1, 1996, p. A1.

Quadagno, Jill. *The Color of Welfare: How Racism Undermined the War on Poverty*. New York and Oxford: Oxford University Press, 1994.

Reich, Charles. "The New Property." *Yale Law Journal* 73 (April 1964): 733–797.

_____. "Individual Rights and Social Welfare." *Yale Law Journal* 74 (June 1965).

Renwick, Trudi, and Barbara Bergmann. "A Budget-Based Definition of Poverty, With an Application to Single-Parent Families." *Journal of Human Resources* 28 (Winter 1993): 1–24.

"Report of the Committee on the Pauper Laws of This Commonwealth" (The Quincy Report). Massachusetts: 1821.

"Report of the Secretary of State on the Relief and Settlement of the Poor" (The Yates Report). New York: 1824.

Rich, Spencer. "Reagan Welfare Proposal Criticized by Agencies." *Washington Post,* February 10, 1987, p. A8.

Rosenbaum, David E. "The Welfare Enigma." *New York Times,* February 10, 1995, p. A16.

Rossiter, Clinton. *The American Presidency.* New York: Harcourt Brace, 1960.

Ruggles, Patricia. *Drawing the Line: Alternative Poverty Measures and Their Implications for Policy.* Washington, DC: Urban Institute Press, 1990.

Segalman, Ralph. "The Protestant Ethic and Social Welfare." *Journal of Social Issues* 24 (1968): 126.

Shear, Jeff. "Looking for a Voice." *National Journal,* March 16, 1996, pp. 591–595.

Shelf, Carl P. *Controversial Issues in Social Welfare Policy.* Newbury Park, CA, London, and New Delhi: Sage Publications, 1992.

"Social Policy. Issue: Welfare." *Congressional Quarterly Special Report,* September 2, 1995, p. 2643.

Stoesz, David. *Small Change: Domestic Policy Under the Clinton Presidency.* White Plains, NY: Longman, 1996.

Thomas, Evan. *Back from the Dead.* New York: Atlantic Monthly Press, 1997.

Thompson, Lyke, and Donald F. Norris. "Introduction: The Politics of Welfare Reform." Chapter 1 in Donald F. Norris and Lyke Thompson, eds., *The Politics of Welfare Reform.* London: Sage Publications, 1995.

Tolchin, Susan. *The Angry American: How Voter Rage Is Changing the Nation.* Boulder: Westview Press, 1996.

Toner, Robin. "War on Overhaul Appears to Be No Contest." *New York Times,* January 13, 1995, p. A25.

_____. "A Six-Decade-Old Policy Is Turned Aside on a Vote of 87 to 12," *New York Times,* September 19, 1995, p. B1.

_____. "Senate Approves Welfare Plan That Would End Aid Guarantee." *New York Times,* September 20, 1995, p. A1.

Trattner, Walter I. *From Poor Law to Welfare State: A History of Social Welfare in America.* 3d ed. New York: Free Press, 1984.

U.S. Congress. House Committee on Ways and Means. *Overview of Entitlement Programs: 1994 Greenbook.* 103rd Congress, 2nd Session, 1994.

Vobejda, Barbara. "Dole Faces GOP Rifts on Welfare." *Washington Post,* September 6, 1995, p. A15.

Vobejda, Barbara, and Judith Havemann. "Conservatives Criticize Dole Welfare Plan." *Washington Post,* August 4, 1995, p. A17.

Weaver, R. Kent. "Controlling Entitlements." Chapter 11 in John E. Chubb and Paul E. Peterson, eds., *The New Direction in American Politics.* Washington, DC: Brookings Institution, 1995.

Wilson, William Julius. *The Truly Disadvantaged: The Inner City, the Underclass, and Public Policy.* Chicago: University of Chicago Press, 1987.

Woodward, Bob. *The Choice.* New York: Simon and Schuster, 1996.

Index